MODERN
Hippie

To everyone who has ever blazed a trail,
making it easier for the rest of us to follow.

MODERN
Hippie

An Intuitive Journey
Toward a Free-Spirited Life

By
Kimberly Kingsley

Published and distributed in the United States by: Intention Love, LLC

For more information about special discounts for bulk purchases, please visit: www.intentionlove.com

Cover and Interior Design: Bryn Starr Best • Cover Photo: Dimitra Kalos • Back Cover Photo: Brandon Tigrett • Editor: Kristine Nally

Library of Congress Cataloging-in-Publication Data

Kingsley, Kimberly A.

Modern Hippie: An Intuitive Journey toward a Free-Spirited Life / Kimberly Kingsley

p. cm.

ISBN 978-0-9964581-0-8

1. Spirituality. 2. Mind/Body I. Title.

Printed in the United States of America

Table of Contents

Introduction

Let's go back in time for a moment and remember the glory days of the classic hippie.

What comes to mind? Long hair parted down the middle, hip hugger jeans, weed—a lot of weed... and other drugs too, all of which seemed to unleash the spirit and invoke a feeling of unbound freedom. I happened to plop down on planet earth just as the flower children were beginning to blossom. My soul somehow knew that this was an important time of cultural change not to be missed. At the heart of this enviable era was a desire for more peace, equality and freedom, but the pursuit of these ideals came with a cost. The drugs destroyed some of these passionate souls, and at times, well-meaning activism bled into divisiveness. Young men and women even lost their lives while trying to create a better America, as in the Freedom Summer of 1964 when three young civil rights activists were murdered while investigating the cause of a church fire in Mississippi. This and other tragedies punctuated the timeline of the movement, which carried inherent risks due to its revolutionary nature. As the '60s rolled into the '70s and the '70s rolled into the '80s, the hippies started building families and careers, and the movement seemed to take a sabbatical. The collective desire for more peace, love and freedom stayed alive though, as desires of the heart never die. They simply go underground until enough people reignite them within their own hearts, and the desire resurfaces into the collective consciousness. The hippies who lived in that era still embody the passion and renegade spirit that demanded peace and shattered rigid race and gender stereotypes. We recognize them as the professors, writers and business people who continue to challenge the status quo and carve out paths, fraught with overgrown and often dying shrubs, making it easier for the rest of us to follow.

And now, the values of this movement have once again bubbled up into the consciousness of those of us who are like-minded. While the essence of the hippie archetype remains intact, the Modern Hippie has a slightly different look and feel, similar to when fashion comes back around with a fresh twist. The classic hippie wore bell bottom jeans, while the Modern Hippie wears boot cut; they're both loose at the bottom, but fit best in their own era. It would be redundant to do exactly what the classic hippies did. They made real progress, embroidering progressive ideas firmly into the fabric of society. We—Modern Hippies—are picking up where they left off, only with a more internal focus. So while the hippies of the '60s were intent on changing the external world by protesting war, fighting for civil rights and promoting equality, today's hippie is intent on changing his or her internal world. It is because we are able to enjoy these external freedoms that we are now ready for an unprecedented level of *inner* freedom—we are ready to be free spirits in the truest sense of the word. The tethers that bind us today are different than those of the '60s. Today we are seeking freedom from attachments to old paradigms, habits, and relationships that are toxic. This still requires a form of activism that seeks peace, but now we're focused on creating peace within our own hearts, minds, and lives, knowing that a spirit is not free when it's at war, whether it is with others or oneself. We are aware that whatever inner peace we are able to cultivate will organically spill over into our relationships, workplace and the society in which we live. We've also learned that taking drugs will not lead to sustainable freedom, so this time around we've decided to stay relatively sober,

3

as the cyclical nature of evolution demands that we take what was courageously started in the '60s to the next level. Along with "saying no to drugs" we're called to stay true to hippie form and refrain from divisiveness by choosing not to demonize those who are different. And even though many of us cluster around certain types of music and various causes that respect other human beings and the earth, not as many of us are marching or protesting. For the Modern Hippie, becoming a true free spirit is primarily a solitary journey.

This book is about my quest to become an authentic free spirit and the insights I've had along the way as a student and teacher of the Truth. I am a member of a fairly large group and we all have a story to tell. Many of our stories overlap, as our challenges are much the same. We are all working to transform relationships that weigh heavily on our spirits. We are all working to honor ourselves more so that we can judge others less. And to honor ourselves we are taking care of our physical bodies because, at the moment, they house our spirit.

While our predecessors were outwardly courageous, we are inwardly courageous, as untangling from that which would strangle our peace can be quite painful, requiring exceptional conviction and determination. But despite the inherent challenges, those of us who have chosen this path know that when all of the dangling pieces of our spirit come back together, we rise to the highest version of ourselves. Like a hot air balloon, the strings that once kept us attached are carefully untied and pulled back so that we are able to freely float above all that once threatened to hold us down. We become whimsical. Spirit dances through us, reaches out and joins with others, follows the fun and elevates everything and everybody in its path. This time around we may not be traveling to Haight-Ashbury in a Volkswagen Bus, but we are on a journey nonetheless. It may even look like we are standing still, but within we are on a crazy, wild road trip! Just like the classic hippies, our trip is fraught with pot holes, detours, road blocks and bad directions, but we are learning to follow our spirit and trust its GPS, making it certain that we will arrive.

Chapter 1

Bound

You would think that being a free spirit would come natural to someone born in the mid-sixties. It did for my two best friends, who had no problem dancing on the table at high school parties and hysterically laughing their skinny, blond heads off. I was neither skinny nor blonde, and the last thing I felt was free. The best way to describe myself would have been bound—wound tight in a ball of self-consciousness under a nice, warm blanket of protective chubbiness. My place seemed to be sitting on the sidelines, simply smiling, as I watched my friends frolic in freedom and drink in the sweet nectar of life.

I don't know about you, but when I picture a free spirit, the '60s hippie comes to mind–uninhibited, long-haired men and women dancing like no one is watching. As I was learning how to walk, many of these iconic hippies were expanding their realities with various mind-altering drugs. Who wouldn't be a free spirit after seeing the world through the eyes of LSD? Drugs or no drugs, I believe they were on to something. Those who weren't making their way to San Francisco for what would become known as the Summer of Love were marching on the East Coast in anti-war and civil rights rallies. My Aunt Shirley was one such peaceful protester who got arrested while standing up for equal rights. Go Aunt Shirley! She's definitely the coolest woman I know. I have fond memories of receiving cards and letters in envelopes that she constructed from scrap paper and other junk mail that she'd collected to repurpose.

These tie-dye wearing free birds were kind enough to pass along both drugs and free love to those of us just starting to come of age in the '70s. In addition to the renegade spirit we inherited, we managed to birth our own legendary era: Disco. Even I could be found on the dance floor when The Hustle came on at our middle school dances. At the first hint of the song, my friends and I would scurry our bell-bottom wearing booties and feathered hair to the dance floor and all move in sync. As long as I was tightly nestled between my two best friends, I was able to settle into the comfort of their shadow and join in. By the time we entered high school, the disco era was in full swing and young people all around the world were dancing under blinding strobe lights and sparkling disco balls.

Despite the glimpses of freedom that I experienced on the dance floor or during laughter-filled sleepovers with my friends, the winter season of my life continued as my spirit remained deep in hibernation, bound up in a corner of my psyche. I wish I could say that there was a good reason for what today's psychologists would call social anxiety, but I wasn't abused or traumatized as a child, I was merely sensitive. I can't even blame it on being chubby, as I wasn't even all that aware of the fat that had amassed to buffer the inexplicable and often painful space between me and my spirit.

While you may or may not relate to feeling like this as a child, chances are you've experienced the need to protect yourself from the world or people around you at some point in your life and responded by pulling your spirit out of harm's way and shielding it for a time. Eventually, however, each of us is called to "find ourselves," but just because we are called to do so doesn't mean that we will. By virtue of the fact that you are holding this book, I would venture to guess that you are one of the brave souls who has answered the call. In this sense we are traveling together on this journey toward becoming a free spirit, or what I like to think of as a Modern Hippie.

In these pages I share my journey—sometimes painful and other times laughable—of moving from bound to free, and I want to take you with me. As a spiritual student and teacher for over twenty years, I've been blessed to receive hundreds of insights, models of healing, and lessons directly from Spirit. I will share many of these as well, but before we go any further, let's take a look at what it means to be a free spirit.

Today's Hippie

What exactly is a Modern Hippie? I view her as today's equivalent of the original hippie. Having experienced everything that has happened since that time, she is clearly her own breed, but maintains the essence of the movement with her unwavering pursuit of peace and freedom. From the outside she looks relaxed. Like water, she's able to go with the flow and easily adapt to change. She's attractive because the source of her beauty comes from the spirit that shines like the sun through each and every one of her cells. She's far from perfect, however, and doesn't try too hard, because trying too hard comes from a place of insecurity, not freedom. This new wave of free spirits may or may not embrace contemporary hippie fashion, as we are supremely focused on inner freedom with the outer symbols being less important. And unlike my teenage daughter's image of a hippie, she's not stinky, overly hairy or unkempt because she takes impeccable care of herself. The Modern Hippie has learned to avoid the often tempting short cuts to freedom because she knows that artificially getting to the top of the mountain most certainly leads to a hard fall as the temporary mountain crumbles from beneath her. She marches to the beat of her own steel drum knowing that, ultimately, her freedom depends on the ability to make choices that are in alignment with her own values. She's not a hater. She has opinions, but easily loves others, even when they think differently. She's passionate because she follows her bliss, whatever that might be. And she's a little eccentric like my Aunt Shirley because no one can be completely themselves without becoming somewhat quirky. She no longer hides behind a curtain of false humility, for she has claimed her gifts. And because of this, she is able to generously acknowledge and appreciate the gifts of others. She is not afraid to say no. She's learned that a yes that should be a no compromises her spirit, ultimately serving no one. You could say that she's powerful, because she is. But it's a power grounded in love. It's not prickly or jagged, but it is fierce. She no longer tolerates anyone trying to mitigate her power because she knows that freedom depends on the ability to house her own energy and that losing her power means losing a piece of herself.

She's not an airy fairy new-ager who lives in the clouds. She lives on this earth and in her body with the knowledge that just as electricity needs grounding to travel, she too needs to keep both feet firmly planted on the ground if her spirit is to soar. She's spontaneous, but not reckless. And because she knows that the feeling of being high is the direct result of spirit moving through her body, she's careful not to make choices that would compromise her own wellbeing.

From an energy perspective, she is untangled. She loves to connect with others and enjoy all that life has to offer but has effectively unraveled from relationship drama, compulsive behaviors and over-consumption. Her freedom is the result of pulling her energy back from all the people, places and things that used to grip her so that her spirit can take its rightful place within her heart, mind and body. And because she's no longer owned by anything or anyone, she is able to love with all her heart, savor every bite of food, and take in each colorful sunset without ever abandoning herself. She is you. And she is me.

What a Modern Hippie is *not* is someone who impulsively does whatever she wants. Spontaneity does not always equal freedom. It depends on what master you're serving. Are you serving your ego's desire for immediate gratification or are you serving the highest part of you? Ironically, total freedom entails being a perfect servant to your own spirit, becoming a disciple, if you will. Only rather than following someone else, we apply our discipline to that which honors our own spirit. At times, Spirit does direct us to take spontaneous action because it only lives in the present, but if we're not mindful, it's easy to deceive ourselves into spontaneously acting from lower impulses.

Right now the hippie archetype has a magnetic pull. It has resurfaced into the collective conscience of society, and many of us highly resonate with the essence of the movement. And now, everything, from the trailblazers of the '60s who boldly unleashed their version of freedom to the more recent self-help movement that has taught millions of us how to live happier, healthier lives, has primed us to take our freedom to the next level.

If you're like me, you've read more books than you can count. You've learned how to set boundaries using "I" statements, and you eat relatively clean. You've meditated, perhaps done your fair share of yoga or Pilates, and have engaged in numerous experiences for the sake of personal growth. The self-help movement has been great, exactly what we needed, but a new era has dawned. The work we've done has brought us to the point where we are ready to trust ourselves and simply live. We've built a solid foundation and have completed most of our own repair work. The only thing left to do is jump into the river of life and allow the rapids to deliver us to the next level of freedom. Don't get me wrong; I still meditate daily and do plenty of yoga. And I'll still pick up a self-help book if it pertains to what I'm interested in at the moment. But it's different now. I'm not reading it as if my life depended on it. I'm reading to hear another perspective from someone I respect. Now, more often than not, when my spirit leads me to a book, it's for the purpose of validating what I already know in my own heart or to give me perspective on a situation that's eluding me.

This is a pivotal point in the growth of humanity. Because of how quickly things are changing, we need to become more agile and intuitive than we ever thought possible. I don't believe it is a choice, but an evolutionary mandate. It's as if we're straddling two worlds, the old world of chasing what we think will bring us fulfillment by setting goals, working hard and competing to get ahead, and the new world of spiritual shape shifting. The only choice is to take a leap of faith and become a shape shifter ourselves, allowing Spirit to rapidly mold us into our best self and transform us often to keep us relevant.

Becoming a Modern Hippie

The journey to freedom is both lifelong and moment-to-moment. Most people I know continue to untangle from habits and relationships that siphon their power. This is certainly true for me, but thankfully, due to a series of synchronistic events and an unwavering commitment to growth, my spirit is now freer than it ever has been. You'd think it would be the other way around. The kid is the free spirit who contracts with each hard knock that life throws his way. Not this kid. I was "sensitive," which was both good and bad. Becoming

15

friends with the various cacti and shrubs that lined the streets on my walk to school each day was cool. The fact that my best friend, Roover, was imaginary and played whatever I wanted while taking complete responsibility for any mishaps that might, and did, occur was great. And, I'm pretty sure this same sensitivity is what allows me to clearly hear the voice of my own spirit, which I genuinely appreciate. However, there is a downside. I was hyper-aware of everything around me. I much preferred playing with my imaginary friend than being bombarded with the energy of thirty wild kindergarteners. My inner world and the company of close family and friends provided a safe haven, but anything beyond that put me into frozen mode where my spirit did not feel safe enough to come out and play. Just about the time I was abruptly lifted out of my peaceful inner world and dropped into the chaotic environment of school, I stumbled upon a friend who ended up helping me a lot. She offered me protection and buffered me from all the chaos. Her name was Food. Food was amazing. I could eat two to three Ding Dongs and be as cool as a cucumber. Cereal did the trick too; it would pour down on my anxiety like rain in the desert. I can feel it now... that sensation of carb-induced calmness. The only problem with using food to treat sensitivity is that by the time I started sixth grade I was officially obese (granted, what we considered obese then is viewed as being only slightly chubby now). Thankfully, my mother stepped in and asked if I wanted help losing weight, and it dawned on me that this might be a good idea. So that summer I went on a "milkshake diet" where I drank a disgusting blend of frozen chalkiness twice a day while eating one healthy meal, a diet for a child that would raise some serious eyebrows today. Nevertheless, it worked. By the end of the summer I'd lost twenty pounds and felt great about myself and really enjoyed sporting a bikini alongside my naturally skinny friends. I thought this might do the trick—freedom at last! But fat was the symptom, not the cause of my inhibitions. Food was the only thing that eased the ache in the pit of my belly that came from knowing that something was missing. I knew that I desperately needed nourishment but had no clue that the only thing that would truly satiate me was my own spirit. Releasing the fat did seem to loosen the knot of my bound spirit, even if ever so slightly. Every now and then, if the wind blew in just the right direction, I would get a whiff of Spirit. I would feel its presence in the form of an insight, a peaceful moment or an uninhibited burst of excitement, and then POOF, it would be gone and I'd be back to my old self. Feeling self-conscious is only the tip of the iceberg though. Because I couldn't feel my spirit, I did what any normal (and by normal, I mean unconscious) person would do. I chased it!

However, we all know this doesn't work. Each attempt to find ourselves in other people, places and things takes us one step further from what we really want—a vibrant, free spirited life. The first third of my life was one long chase. Of course, the objects (or subjects) of my chase would vary, but the pursuit was unwavering. I continuously projected my buried spirit onto various forms (first food, then boys…), then dizzily ran toward the recipient of my projection without ever taking a breath.

My chase ensued for nearly three decades, long enough for me to become a full-fledged neurotic mess. I continued to have a fucked up relationship with food and hence my body. And although I loved men, I didn't love myself enough to know how to pick them... Nor did I trust myself. I desperately needed some kind of foundation. I was like the bird in the classic children's book going around asking all the other animals, "Are you my mother?" I didn't know who I was and I didn't know how to find out. When you don't have a foundation, a lot of solace can be found in the concrete energy of food. What comforted me as a child ended up terrorizing me as a young adult. Early on food did help to buffer my sensitivity, but as I got older and more interested in my appearance, I swapped over-eating for restricted eating. Eventually I developed a quasi eating disorder. My life had become overrun with control and obsessive thinking. Once or twice a week, my restrictive eating would give way to a carb fest. These routine binge sessions kept me in a cycle of perpetual guilt followed by ego driven determination to not mess up again... It never ended well. My will to eat right wasn't grounded in authentic power; therefore, I had no willpower.

At the time, I was working as an inside sales rep for a manufacturing company. My life became like the movie Ground Hog Day. Every morning before heading off to work, I ate a couple of bialys (a lighter version of a bagel) topped with fat free cottage cheese and jam. I declined any lunch invitations in favor of a solo fat-free frozen yogurt. Remember when dieting was all about fat free food? Yuck! After work, I went to the gym and jumped on the elliptical machine for about 45 minutes. On the days I "ate well," I skipped dinner only to wake up the next morning and do it all over again. But control is a form of avoidance, and one can only stuff her feelings and avoid the call of her spirit for so long before the pent up energy turns against her. The restless energy that was bound up within me soon turned into anxiety as it began to rumble louder in order to get my attention. Prozac hadn't yet become a household name, and no one would have considered putting a neurotic young woman on meds anyway. I lived in an obsession factory, spinning in endless circles around things that didn't matter. I felt deeply restless most of the time and had no sense of who I was. It was like living in a pressure cooker with a broken latch that could blow at any moment. When panic washed over me at work one day for no reason at all, I knew that something had to give. I remember thinking *I've got to get out of here or I'm going to die.*

The Voice of My Spirit

Soon after the panic incident, I learned that my cousin was moving to Chicago. I thought about moving with her, but couldn't make sense of quitting a secure job and leaving my family and friends. Then one night after a run when my mind was clear and my heart open, I received an answer to my question. I heard the words, *"You have to go work on yourself so that you can love others more."* I knew this voice was me, but it was also bigger than I was and I trusted it implicitly. The message was so strong that it gave me the conviction and courage that I needed to quit my job and move to Chicago.

Staying in Phoenix was not an option. My increasingly bound and pressurized spirit gave me two very clear choices: either go or blow. And in the midst of my desperation, very specific instructions on how to get out were revealed, which meant leaving everything that was familiar or staying and becoming sick.

My mother offered to accompany me on the drive across country; so several weeks later, we packed up my car and headed east. I'm the oldest of four, so spending one on one time with my mom was sacred. We talked and laughed and took in the sites, creating memories that I will carry in my heart for all time.

21

Chapter 2

A Glimpse of Freedom

By the time I arrived in Chicago, my cousin had rented an apartment on the fourth floor of an old brownstone building, less than a block from Lake Michigan. The place was not fancy but quaint, having dark hardwood floors, two small bedrooms, one bathroom, and a radiator for heat—something I'd had no experience with coming from Arizona. Big windows opened to the grassy courtyard below bringing in precious light from the shrinking days. The cold from the brisk October wind penetrated my bones, piercing through my coat like tiny ice picks and chipping away the façade that had become my identity. It seemed like the wind slapped me across the face and yelled, "Wake-up!" My unconscious slumber was about to come to an abrupt halt.

It's said that when the student is ready the teacher will come. With my comforts gone and my senses open, I was ready. A teacher can come in any form—he, she, or it acts as a messenger of the truth, reminding you of what you already know but are only now ready to remember. You can hear a message a thousand times, but if you're not ready to receive it, you will not recognize it as truth. The very moment you are ready, you will be drawn to whomever or whatever teaches the exact thing that you need to learn. The message will reverberate throughout your body as truth. You will feel validated, ignited and uplifted within yourself.

For me, the teacher came in the form of a newly released book called, *A Return to Love* by Marianne Williamson, which is based on another set of books called *A Course in Miracles (The Course)*. The message in the book was simple: God is love. What is common knowledge for us today was revolutionary then, ultimately reaching millions of people who, like me, were starving for a message that made sense. The book prompted a mass spiritual awakening, of which I am honored to be a part.

For the first time ever I was able to see the bigger picture—that life is meant to move through us and beyond us rather than be chased and manipulated in order to feed the ego's version of ideal. Talk about divine intervention—as soon as my defenses were stripped, life shot an arrow of truth into the center of my heart that changed everything. At that moment my spirit aroused from a long, deep sleep and began to rise up within me and fill me with the love I'd been chasing all those years. The day I picked up *A Return to Love*, I started reading feverishly, knowing in my bones that it contained something that I desperately needed to know. Within hours I began to cry. Tears of relief rolled down my cheeks for three days. I cried at night and in the morning, I cried on the bus on my way to work and I cried on my way home. The crying seemed to be in direct proportion to the fear and tension I'd been holding all those years and each tear I shed made me a little lighter. I was finally able to relax and know that, as Bob Marley would say, "Every little thing is gonna be alright."

No wonder I'd been afraid. Until that point, I was living in Opposite Land where life is consumed, rather than expressed. Even though I was still farther away from being a free spirit than I could have ever imagined, a thousand years of confusion was lifted from my psyche. It wasn't just my confusion; this was society's conglomeration of fucked-up platitudes that brainwash us into believing that we are only as good as we look and worth only the amount of money listed on our bank statement. None of this makes any sense. My thoughts started to shift. "Oh, I don't need to be perfect. I don't need to chase life. I don't need to swim round and round in my head, never getting anywhere." I began to notice that when I allowed life to move through me, I felt inner peace and freedom, but when I forgot to be a vessel for Spirit, I'd return to chasing it and quickly slip back into a state of pressure, anxiety and uncertainty.

Over the course of the following year, I took countless walks around my Chicago neighborhood and along Lake Michigan. The lake was my inspiration. It was wild and free like my spirit. But becoming a Modern Hippie with a spirit that freely flows into the world doesn't happen by simply knowing the truth. Yes, my spirit was awake and I knew that this was the beginning of something huge, but true freedom—spirit that's wild, free and gracefully flowing—requires aligning every thought, relationship, habit and intention with Spirit's purpose rather than the ego's. But because of beginner's luck or perhaps the grace of God, the magnitude of this realization made me feel on top of the world, like nothing could bring me down or steal my peace ever again. At the time, I believed that my transformation was complete, and on one level it was. My foundation was set, never to be shaken again. I also received conviction that my life's purpose was to teach these principles. I couldn't live with myself knowing how many people were still living in Opposite Land where they had forgotten that their function was to extend, not to chase, Spirit.

The Windy City is a mystical place. I'm not sure which is more powerful, the huge expanse of water cradling the city or the wind that blows everything clean, but it transformed me into an open being who could no longer block the massive life energy that was trying to rise up within me. Like Sleeping Beauty, it took the kiss of love to wake me up and now it was time to go through a complete reorganization in preparation for the immense amount of Spirit that was about to extend through me. Upon finishing *A Return to Love*, I purchased *A Course in Miracles* and began the daily lessons in the workbook. Each day I would affirm a different truth such as:

> *I have given everything I see in this room (on this street, from this window, in this place) all the meaning that it has for me.*

None of it made sense at the time, but The Course doesn't ask that you believe it, only that you complete each of the 365 lessons. Upon completing the workbook, one is considered to be a teacher of God. The Course acknowledges that there are many paths and that anyone can become a teacher of God if they choose. But it also states that while the call is universal and many people hear it, few will answer.

I answered the call in the moment that I listened to my spirit and decided to move to Chicago. Had I not done so, I'm certain that I would have remained a hot mess for the rest of my days. I would be addicted to something or someone, exhausted from the unending pursuit, and in desperate need of validation for my very existence. To me, being a teacher of God only means that you have successfully shifted your point of reference from your ego to your spirit, no longer chasing whatever you thought would make you happy, but instead, extending the love that you are into the world. Those who are able to demonstrate this level of inside-out living are teachers by their presence alone. Others recognize the inner peace of the teacher and become inspired to find peace for themselves. You may well be a teacher of God too, but more important than the title is the direction in which we are moving.

The reversal from consuming life to express-ing life is a process and a journey. Whether you are just now answering the call or if you answered it decades ago doesn't matter, once your spirit has been given permission to rise up within you, it leads the way and your destiny is certain. I honor whatever path you have chosen and the process that has brought you to this point in your journey.

Life in the City

While I would have loved to remain in LaLa Land for the rest of my days, walking to the lake with my coffee and writing in my journal, my sav-ings had run out and I needed a job. Each day I'd get on the bus and head downtown via Michigan Avenue. I always tried to get a window seat so that I could watch the waves of the lake dancing wildly in the wind. With my journal still in hand, I'd write down every insight that came to me. This was an invigorating time, but I have to acknowl-edge that being in a highly spiritual state is not ideal for job hunting. During one interview, I was asked about my biggest weakness. Fumbling for an answer, I finally uttered, "I don't know."

The man interviewing me responded abruptly, "Well, come back when you do." Note to self:

Remember to come down from the clouds and enter your body before an interview!

I finally got a job selling copy services, which entailed visiting law firms, introducing myself and seeing if they needed copy services. Easy enough, right? The "No Soliciting" signs made me a little nervous, but I was told to ignore them and make my sales pitch to the receptionist anyway. Things went from bad to worse the day I walked right by a No Soliciting sign and asked the receptionist if they were in need of copy services. Without saying a word, she picked up the phone and called someone. I got so excited and couldn't believe that she was calling someone to come speak to me about the company's copy needs. Next thing I know, a

security guard walks into the office and says, "Come with me." Without even looking in my eyes, he leads me to a big freight elevator that's dark and dirty. He motions for me to get in.

"What? Can't I just go down the regular elevator?"

"No—you need to leave this way," he uttered, without a hint of warmth in his voice. Having been sheltered and treated like a princess my entire life, I was devastated. I almost burst into tears in that elevator and vowed never to make another cold call for the rest of my life.

The next day I told my boss what happened, thanked her for the opportunity and quit my job. Her response shocked me. "You can't quit! You're the only other woman in the office that I can relate to." I thanked her for caring but was adamant about never getting humiliated again.

"You don't even have to sell..." She whispered. "Just come in each morning and leave the office as if you're going out to make sales calls. In the meantime, we'll continue to pay your base salary."

I told her that I didn't feel right about that, but she assured me that as part owner she had the authority to make that decision. I ended up agreeing and spending the next several months exploring downtown Chicago, my journal still in one hand and a Starbucks coffee in the other. How did this happen? How did I manage to get paid to study spirituality? I traversed every nook and cranny of that gorgeous and sometimes gritty city. One day, while waiting for the bus, I met a homeless man. He was not much older than me and he was handsome even through his long, dirty hair and baggy clothes. "Why are you homeless?" I asked. He looked at me with love, as if it had been a while since anyone even cared.

"I don't know" is all he said. But we had a human moment and for that I'm grateful.

Ironically, I later started dating an attorney who owned a successful law firm located in downtown Chicago. We met at *A Course in Miracles* study group and shared a passion for spirituality. Had I met him while still working at the copy center, he would have gladly given me his firm's copying business, but then my experience would have been completely different. I wouldn't have had the opportunity to simply wander the city and integrate my new learning, and as a spiritual newborn, this gift of time was a true blessing.

I continued to study The Course and would complete the workbook in a little over a year, upon which time my teacher/guru shifted from The Course to the spirit within me that began to direct my every move. Sometimes the direction would be subtle and other times I would hear an audible voice. My intuition started to blossom and I began to receive my own insights. One of the first was a model of health and healing that I call The Container Theory. It is the basis for my first book, *Opening to Life,* and to this day I share it with my students at the college where I teach.

Container Theory

It is simple, as all truth is, and illustrates the levels of self and their order of importance. Each of us is a container for spirit; some are solid, some are cracked and others are severely broken. Regardless, our task is to repair our own container so that we are strong enough to receive, contain and express the intense energy of spirit. There are those who have permanently broken their container by forcing spirit through an unprepared vessel using drugs or other mind-altering techniques. When this happens, one becomes psychotic and loses a cohesive sense of identity. This is when we hear people claiming to be Jesus Christ and others. Who knows what's real and what's not with these people. The problem is that in a state of psychosis one is unable to function. Our container needs to be strengthened over time in order to channel such raw power without crumbling. Some people have very little repair work to do. Perhaps they grew up in an environment that supported emotional, mental and physical health and continued to make life-enhancing choices as they came of age and grew into adulthood. The time it takes one to strengthen one's container varies, but for me it's taken years—decades—to be able to channel my spirit freely. It's still a work in progress—this process of enlightenment. In those first few years I was more of a wounded warrior than a Modern Hippie. I had just come out of battle with myself and could see the light at the end of the tunnel but would have a long, long way to go before I could *be* the light. The initial spiritual knowledge and conviction that came to me was only the tip of the iceberg, but it was strong enough to keep me focused and I never looked back.

Strengthening one's container involves repairing energetic holes that develop as a result of our instant gratification habits of consumption. Most people don't know this, but every time we soothe ourselves by unconsciously over-consuming, we compromise the integrity of our container. If we do it too many times, it creates a vortex or a hole that isn't supposed to be there. So rather than spiritual energy organically rising up from within and cohesively flowing into the world, the energy fragments and disperses through the holes in one's container. This further weakens us and stunts our growth. Repair on this level involves processing old emotion (the reason we engage in self-defeating behavior in the first place) and then changing our behaviors to what we know is right for our own evolution. The self-discipline required to change can be hard to come by though, as it's difficult to muster up the willpower without being anchored in the conviction that spiritual energy is a thousand times more fulfilling than whatever immediate gratification behavior is tempting us at the moment. We have to somehow learn—for me it was through The Course—that Spirit isn't a servant to us, but we to it. Spirit is our foundation and our primary level of being and the other levels of self—emotional, mental and physical—need to support the goal of spiritual expression.

On the level of thought, this involves a literal reversal in thinking from what we are taught in society. Society tells us to chase our dreams, to compete for what we want. Society tells us that when one person wins, another loses, and that someone else's good fortune, beauty or fame lowers our chances of achieving the same. We're taught that we have to build up our egos and defend ourselves lest we get eaten alive. And until we learn the truth about who we are and how we're meant to function as healthy human beings, we are deeply confused, possibly turning to medication to "fix" us and make us feel better. Compounding the inherent challenges of personal transformation is that these beliefs and emotions are free floating in our environment and seem to seep in without us even knowing it. We have to retrain ourselves to remain centered in our own being and to know that at the level of spirit, we are all connected. Some people, much like me when I was twenty, simply don't know the laws of life. The only real difference between human beings is the degree to which we are able to receive, contain and express Spirit. It's impossible to chase it (in the form of whatever we think will make us happy) and express it at the same time. Chasing anything means that we have forgotten who we are and need to re-center, receive and know that we will be led to the next right thing. The more any of us can do our part in turning our upside down world right side up, the easier we make it for others to do the same.

The container theory became my metaphor and model for healing. Once we connect with our spirit, clear out old, heavy emotion, align our thoughts with the expressive nature of life, and treat our body like the sacred vessel that it is, Spirit is able to effectively lead us to our highest life.

Time to Go Home

A year into my Chicago pilgrimage, I learned that Deepak Chopra was speaking at a spiritual conference downtown. At that time, he wasn't the superstar guru that he is today. But I had read his book, *Perfect Health,* and was excited to hear what he had to say. The morning of the conference I put on my favorite purple dress and took the bus downtown. I arrive early and place my sweater on a seat to save it before taking a walk outside. Just as I exit the building I spot Chopra walking down the street with a tall gentleman. Excitement overtakes me and I turn and walk in his direction. As they approach, I look up at Chopra with big eyes and an innocent smile and say hello. Having been through this a time or two, the men are gracious and welcoming. The tall gentleman asks my name. I tell him and then look back to Chopra. Then the tall gentleman asks if I'm attending the conference. "Yes," I say, and again, look back to Chopra.

After several of these exchanges, I turn to the tall gentleman and say, "I'm sorry sir, but I don't know who you are." They both burst out laughing, and then the tall gentleman proceeds to introduce himself as Wayne Dyer. I'm sure this was a defining moment, as Dr. Dyer had been on the scene for many years and Chopra was a relative newcomer. After the laughter subsided, Chopra kindly asked me a few questions, and then we said our goodbyes.

As I walked away tears began to flow down my face. They were the strangest tears I've ever shed. They didn't come from sadness or even joy—they were a physical reaction to the spiritual presence of these two men. I've since heard that these types of reactions can occur when you encounter the strong presence of God in another.

Later, Chopra gave an inspiring talk about the nature of spirit and the connection between mind and body. At the end, he led us in a group meditation. Groups of people tend to increase the power of meditation, so I found myself quickly dipping into the sacred space within. From within this sea of silence I hear my inner voice once again. This time it says, "You are on your path now, you might as well go home where people love you." The same voice that urged me to move in the first place now gave me permission to end my pilgrimage, go home and start my life as a teacher of God.

A year could have been a lifetime. Nothing about me was the same as when I had arrived in Chicago. Prior to leaving the glorious city where I found my spirit, I decide to take one more solo walk along Lake Michigan. I find myself so overwhelmed with love and gratitude that my walk is more like a prance. In the midst of what feels like communion with the divine, I silently say, "I love you Jesus." Then to my surprise, I hear "I love you too" as if he were walking right next to me. The familiar tears of awakening stream down my face as I realize that, in fact, he is.

Descending from the Mountain

Going home provided me a *big* dose of reality. I had assumed I was good to go, that nothing or no one could ever again steal my peace, that I would be on a perpetual high for the rest of my days.

Then I landed in Phoenix.

I'm sure I'm not the only one to leave home, grow up and then return only to have the same family dynamics bring out their inner ten-year-old. I came back to a city full of associations to the old Kim—the same family, friends and places I'd been my entire life. Assuming my move would be a lateral one, I was stunned to find myself back at the bottom of the mountain. I'd had the mountaintop experience, but didn't yet live there. In order to be there all the time, I would have to further anchor myself into my now toddler spirit while going through all the trials and tribulations that everyone has to go through on the hero's journey.

My growth seemed to slow to a near halt, and instead of moving forward I felt like I was moving in old familiar circles. My apparent stagnation had nothing to do with the people or location, but rather the familiar grooves of relating that were so natural and automatic. Every single area of my life needed to be exposed to this new light of awareness and reorganized to align with it. Starting with my perception—the way I viewed myself and the world—then extending to my behaviors. Eventually every cell of my body and every aspect of my being would have to undergo the Inner Peace Test. If I didn't experience inner peace around a specific area, it meant that Spirit wasn't flowing and I either had emotional blocks or was out of alignment.

The process of refinement would go something like this: I'd bump into anxiety, resistance or judgment, and I would need to pray to see the situation through the eyes of my spirit. Sometimes my perception would instantly shift and I would feel peace. Other times, especially with food and men, the familiar grooves would be so deep, the blocks so immense, and the attachments so tangled that I would have to sit in the fire long enough for spirit to burn through the pattern. Not just once, but over and over again. Entering the fire of transformation is not fun, and likely the exact reason why it's sometimes easier to distract oneself from growth. In some cases, bringing a pattern to the light of awareness took years. On one level I was whole. My spirit was awake and I was aware of my essential nature. I was clear on my purpose of allowing spirit to flow through me and was committed to living my highest life while teaching these principles to others. But even with all this clarity, the emotional, mental and physical parts of me were not yet on board.

I speak as if these other areas have a mind of their own, and in my experience they do. Until aligned with one's highest self, the other levels of self seem to have their own agenda. In my case, my emotional self was still thirteen. It was still seeking attention and approval and tended to throw a tantrum (usually a quiet one) when it didn't get its way. I was loaded with heavy, sticky, unprocessed emotion that lived underground the vast majority of the time, only to erupt within me when triggered. Somehow during mountain top experiences, grace allows us to bypass our emotional landfill and just receive love, insight or however Spirit chooses to reveal itself. I had received a full year of emotional bypassing. I figured all of my issues had been magically removed during my awakening.

Although my emotions were in serious need of maturation, affirming the lessons from The Course had begun to reorganize my thoughts to be more in line with reality. Even so, I needed much more practice. My thoughts remained undisciplined and continued to engage in an active partnership with my emotional self to reinforce patterns of ego driven negativity.

I was connected to the source of my spirit the way a river is connected to a large body of water, but my spirit was still too dammed up and fragmented to flow, as it was continuously diverted into patterns of self-doubt and judgments about myself and others. My body had not become the clear vessel for Spirit that it needed to be either. After a decade of calorie restriction, I went wild and ate everything in sight. Once I realized my spiritual nature, I no longer felt compelled to "control" my eating. (Note to self: the pendulum always swings back). This would lead to a whopping twenty pound weight gain that year, and on my 5'4" frame, that's a lot. Not attractive, but progress nonetheless. So while I was on the right track on every level, a lot of integration had to occur. And although I had previously thought my work was over, in reality it had just begun. Awareness alone is never enough; it's like turning a light on, but once the light is on, every nook and cranny within one's psyche needs to be brought to the light and transformed or released. Only then can we be internally free—a Modern Hippie.

Chapter 3

Untangling

What inspires me about the original hippies was their ability to be so whimsical. What is it about these free birds that allowed them to move through life so gracefully? Their bright, flowing clothes seemed to be a natural extension of their spirit's vibrant flow. Perhaps like the snapshot many of us have of the decadent, dance-filled roaring '20s, stories of the 1960s seem to suggest that the hippies danced however the music moved them, loved whoever felt right at the moment and traveled wherever the road took them. For some, the essence of this movement may appear irresponsible, but to me, this level of freedom is enviable. I probably envy this approach to life because of my opposite tendency to cling to relationships so tightly that I become tangled up in their energy and linger way longer than is good for me, despite the fact that the relationship umbrella had holes and no longer provided the shelter or protection I was seeking. I met my first serious boyfriend as a teenager. It was passionate, young love, and he was as handsome and charming as a boy could be. Let's just say I wasn't the only girl interested in him, and being an equal opportunity lover, he wasn't about to turn away the other girls standing in line. Hey, it was the 1970s; what do you expect? But he assured me that the rumors I was hearing were false and that I was, and always would be, his number one. He would say, "Baby, you know the truth...you're fine, one of a kind, and all mine."

This kind of sweet talking kept me tethered to him for fifteen years—in an up and down, bungee jumping sort of way. Each time I tried to walk away, the intensity of our young love would yank me back and a new shot of adrenalin would carry us forward until the next break up. Fifteen years! What young girl does that? We'll call him Man #1. I recently ran into him and he's still as handsome and charming as ever, but he has turned over a new leaf. He's now committed to his faith and his own growth. #proudofhim. One never knows where these strong attachments come from. There was nothing in my stable, suburban upbringing that would have lended itself to such a dramatic and unstable relationship.

Shortly after moving back from Chicago I met the man who would become my husband. We'll call him Man #2. The first time I saw him I was walking with my friend, and he jogged by us and said hello. I turned to my friend and said, "Nice legs!" He was 6'4", lean, and later I would learn has a Scottish accent. SOLD! Around the time Braveheart was released, I decided to marry him. He didn't cheat, which was a step up, but his combination of aloofness with my tendency to over-attach made us a pretty combustible couple. By the time our relationship ended there was nothing left but ash and smoke. And although I didn't take walking away from a marriage lightly, it was the right thing to do. The relationship lasted seven years. And while the writing was on the wall years one, two and three, I wouldn't have had my beautiful baby girl had we ended sooner. We've successfully raised her together for sixteen years. #noregrets.

Seven years after my divorce I was in the groove of raising my daughter, teaching, and writing when man #3 came along. I resisted getting into another relationship, but this man was relentless. I was a tough nut to crack, but eventually he would re-open my heart. And despite enjoying a level of stability that I hadn't experienced until that point, we never arrived at a place of mutual readiness. When one was ready to commit, the other was not. In retrospect, it's clear that we were never a long-term match, but sometimes relationships are designed for growth rather than longevity. When our paths diverged nearly five years later, we said our goodbyes. #makingprogress.

No relationship is a waste of time. They've each given me the opportunity to become clear about who I am and what I deserve. They've helped me learn how to handle my emotions and express them appropriately. (I know, I sound like a counselor here, but I am, so bear with me...) I've left out the gritty details because I've already grieved, processed and moved on from each of these pivotal relationships, and my real interest here is to reflect on how each man helped me untangle a little more from my own binding patterns and move toward freedom within myself and within the context of a relationship. Of course, growth doesn't come without pain, and there is a lot of pain between the lines of what I've written. But as I became stronger within myself, honoring my spirit became easier. Am I learning how to release what isn't right more quickly? Am I becoming more like a Modern Hippie—more attached to my own soul than the comforts of companionship? The short answer is YES. I love being untangled, as it creates the right environment for Spirit to organically flow, leaving in its wake what The Eagles call, "that peaceful, easy feeling."

To become a Modern Hippie we need to learn how to release attachments to anyone who chronically siphons our spirit. This involves untangling all the ribbons of energy that bind the relationship in a state of unhealthy togetherness and reintegrating the fragmented pieces of one's spirit back into the body. The right relationship is a spiritual dance—an exchange of energy that feels nourishing most of the time. When there are too many days, months or years of energy loss, there's a problem. This is a sign that we are tangled up in relational patterns that constrict spiritual flow. Except under extreme circumstances such as violence, addiction or ongoing dishonesty, I don't believe in ending a relationship before examining your contribution to the dynamic. That's a sure way to end up in the very same dance with a different partner. But once you've identified your part and made necessary changes, it's your partner's turn to do the same. And if he's unwilling, it's time to move on. Of course, you could stay, but then you would be more like a slave to security than a servant to your

spirit. I'm not judging anyone who chooses security, for we each have our own path and lessons,
but my path—and I believe I have some poetic
license here—is freedom. Ideally, freedom within
a loving relationship, but my spirit is my priority
this time around; so if the relationship is not right,
I'm moving on.

Dear God, I Need a Miracle

Examining oneself in the context of a relationship is tricky. Often the easiest thing to do is blame
one's partner when things go awry, but in order
to be spiritually free, we need to take complete
responsibility for our perceptions and our peace.
A Course in Miracles states that misperceptions
are the source of all pain and can be transformed
in an instant simply by asking for a miracle. An
immediate shift to true vision and inner peace is
what we want when we're in an emotional knot,
is it not? When I returned home from my Chicago
pilgrimage I was able to apply this liberating prin-
ciple with relative ease, but once I fell in love with
Man #2, asking for a miracle was, well, like asking
for a miracle. In the throes of an emotional trig-
ger, not only did asking for a miracle not work in
the slightest, it seemed to make things worse! No

wave of peace or liberating insight followed my plea. And on top of my emotional frenzy, I would become upset about why my prayer seemed to fall on deaf ears. This was a very confusing time for me, as I fully believed (and still do) in the principles taught in *The Course*.

What followed this time of hellish confusion was about a five year period of reconciling spiritual principles with material law. I had to figure out why a miracle, which *The Course* defines as a shift in perception, only worked some of the time—the times when I didn't desperately need one... I'll never forget sitting on the couch in the living room one night after having a horrible fight with my soon to be husband. I closed my tear drenched eyes and silently asked for a miracle. Nothing happened. I continued to suffer, thinking, thinking and thinking, feeling distraught and confused. Why, when sadness and frustration had exploded in my body, didn't a miracle lift me out of my misery? Why did the emotion linger within me like leaking radiation in a pool of water? After many months of soul searching, I discovered the one word that most describes this apparent contradiction: Preparation. Who among us becomes enlightened without going through the fire of transformation?

As a seeker and teacher of spiritual truths (and so I wouldn't lose my mind), I continued to flush out the dynamics between these two opposing forces—the instant spiritual healing that I believed was available to me versus the intense emotional turmoil that I was experiencing. I began to slowly grasp the literal nature of energy: how spirit acts instantly and perceives the truth with radical clarity (a miracle), how pent up emotion sits on top of it, often suffocating the very reality that would liberate us, and how our thoughts race in circles trying to make sense of a situation that is often nonsensical. A stark reality began to dawn on me as I came to terms with the fact that I would need to get out of my own way so that Spirit could effectively lead and help me lift this heavy layer of old emotion. But how does one clear emotion that seems as vast as Lake Michigan? Embedded in the word preparation is reparation, which is exactly what needed to happen for me to become clear enough to instantly receive a miracle. I needed to repair my spiritual container, which was quite damaged, so that it would be strong enough for me to finally process and cast off the long-standing emotion that inhibited my spirit.

I began to sense that the emotional energy that I desperately wanted to clear was renewing itself through impulsive behavior. In other words, if I really wanted to release it, I'd need to take a cold, hard look at how I was acting. And what I found is that instead of entering the fire of transformation and allowing the old emotion to be burned off, I prematurely released it by stirring up conflict. I'd vent and cry and talk until the pressure dissipated enough so that I could get on with my day. The only problem with this approach is that it creates holes in one's energy system, releasing the pressure but not the emotion, all the while preventing one from evolving—great for someone who unconsciously wants some relief, but not great for a young woman who's on the fast track to spiritual freedom.

It became clear that if I was to evolve, I'd need to learn to sit in the fire long enough for my spirit to burn through old emotion and strengthen my container. As always, once I was ready, my spirit guided me. I learned to hold on to my emotions when all I wanted to do was spew them onto the man sitting next to me. When I was successful, I'd prevent myself from engaging in conflict, allowing a piece of old emotion to become refined enough to move through my consciousness. Holding on to emotion when you're used to expulsing it in a state of hysterical frenzy is as counter-intuitive as being told to breathe instead of push when you're having a baby. You desperately want to push, but your body needs to go through the pain of contractions in order to move the baby from the uterus to the birth canal. The same is true with emotion, spewing it out prematurely damages our spiritual container; we need to give the raw emotion time to become refined enough to pass through our awareness organically.

In order to grow, I had to get more comfortable with the discomfort of emotional processing. Every time I willingly entered the fire of my intense emotions instead of acting them out, I became a little lighter and clearer, and eventually I was able to receive the miracles that are always available to us. The increasing clarity not only allowed me to more readily accept the peace that was ever present, but once I had sufficiently examined my patterns and strengthened my emotionally weakened container, I was finally given the spiritual clarity and conviction that I needed to walk away from my perennially unhealthy relationship.

Until we do our own work, we remain stuck and confused. I will always have peace about that relationship ending because I completed my spiritual assignment to grow while I was still with him. Had I not entered the fire and strengthened my container by learning how to sit with uncomfortable emotions instead of acting them out, I wouldn't have received clarity and conviction that ending the relationship was the right thing to do. And if I had left prior to doing my own work, I would have simply attracted the same dynamic in another man.

Stepping Out of the Past

While leaving a relationship is sometimes the right thing to do, walking away from what's familiar and comfortable is way easier said than done and requires being vulnerable. You know the feeling when you've recently ended a relationship but haven't yet filled the gap with your own spirit? The space feels as vacant as the chair across from you at the dinner table. You just want to reach out to an ex—any ex—and spend a little time with him. The last time this happened to me, I was in the process of contemplating which ex to text, when I had an epiphany. I heard myself say, "I'm not going backwards." I vowed to stay in the void, not allowing myself to think about anyone from my past.

In the moment that I consciously chose to move forward, I had a vision. I saw and felt myself literally step out of an old version of me. It was about a two inch layer of old feelings and beliefs mixed in with some fat. This layer was comfortable and familiar but was preventing a fresher, freer version of myself from emerging. It was as if I was wearing a spacesuit that unzipped so that I could step out of it if I chose, which I did. I immediately felt lighter and not compelled to think old thoughts that were no longer relevant or useful for my spirit. Each time throughout the day when I was tempted to think about my past, I chose to step out of my old self again.

I believe we are meant to periodically shed and untangle, not only from others, but from our own feelings and beliefs that weigh us down. This is not a comfortable process though! It's way easier to hold on to what's familiar instead of stepping into the unknown. It's like taking your clothes off and just standing there naked until you once again become comfortable in your own skin. It's tempting to just throw something on even if it's too tight or a bit dowdy. But how is one's spirit supposed to dance toward the next perfect thing if it is all bound up in something imperfect? Herein lies a huge piece of the free spirit formula: *Let go of what no longer fits and be willing to stand naked until the next right thing becomes obvious.*

All you have to do is watch some footage of Woodstock to see that hippies knew how to be naked. The Modern Hippie is taking the baton, running with it, and learning how to be emotionally naked. Until we are willing to release attachments and step out of our comfort zone, our spirit will remain bound. The comfortable, warm space suit will stay perfectly intact as long as it gets regular doses of emotional energy. Text an ex? Bam, you get a solid dose of emotional energy to feed your suit. Engage in some good old-fashioned emotional eating, and your suit feels fat and happy for a few days. Throw yourself a pity party and you'll pump yourself up good. Releasing external attachments is only the first step. I've known people who have stepped out of a bad relationship but held the suitcase of bitterness close to their chest, never putting it down.

We have to take the next step and unwind from our internal habit of feeding heavy thoughts with emotion. A thought or belief that is no longer fueled by emotion will simply fade. But we often don't allow that. We pump our old beliefs full of emotion on a regular basis to keep them alive so that we remain comfortably snug in our spacesuit. This isn't freedom! It's false security and I've had enough of it to last my entire life. I'm choosing to get naked, to trade my spacesuit for real security—the kind that comes from being grounded in your own soul.

Shedding and reclaiming our spirit from external attachments grounds us to the point where we can be free without losing our center. Remember the inflatable clowns from childhood that were filled with sand at the bottom? You could punch them all you wanted and they would bounce right back up. That's what it's like to reclaim all of the dangling pieces of your spirit and firmly reattach them to the ground of your being. Nothing can knock you off your center. You might feel thrown off your center for a moment, but before you know it you've bounced back up and moved on. I'm all for healthy attachments—loving connections with others that are loose enough to allow for variation and change. This has a completely different feel than attachments that have become tangled due to chronic power struggles and people trying to manipulate one another.

Spirit is dynamic. It changes form. Partners leave, kids move away, loved ones pass on. We're always going to grieve a loss regardless of the nature of the relationship; however, gripping another person super tight and becoming tangled-up with them is irrational from Spirit's point of view. That said, we've all wrapped our arms and legs around a comfortable but chaotic relationship, so where does our tendency to irrationally attach to others come from?

For some, unhealthy attachments stem from childhood, perhaps due to an abusive or unavailable parent. Some of us hold on too tight to others because we don't see the inherent value within ourselves. For me, and I believe for many of us, these irrational attachments stem from unfinished business...

Do You Believe?

After my spiritual awakening I remember a friend asking me what I thought about reincarnation. "I find the whole concept of reincarnation irrelevant... Why should we distract ourselves with the past when we have to do the work in the present anyway?"

"Well, don't you think it's fascinating?" she asks, seeming perplexed that I didn't share her enthusiasm. We drill down on the topic as we normally do with these things, but my position didn't change. I just couldn't see the point.

Not long after that conversation, I was led to attend a talk from psychiatrist and past life regression expert, Brian Weiss. As a therapist myself, I was curious about his theories and thought I might get some tips for working with my own clients. He did share a little about his professional experience, which was fascinating, but then quickly launched into a group regression! Before I could talk myself out of it, my eyes were closed and I was headed on a journey to my past. Once I arrived, a dramatic scene unfolded where I was the main character in what felt like a tragic drama. As the main character, I experienced the scene first hand, feeling every feeling with acute sensitivity. It begins with me walking into a formal rose garden that's adjacent to a sprawling, white, two-story colonial home somewhere in the Southern United States. The immediate grounds are expansive and well manicured, surrounded by tall trees and lush green in every direction. Inhaling the scent of sweet smelling flowers, I take a seat on one of the two white plaster benches that sit on the edge of the garden. The sky is deep blue and I feel a cool breeze brush over my skin. Peace washes over me as the power of nature lures me into its stillness.

My dress is white. It looks like it's from the 1800s; it is fitted on top with a skirt that goes all the way to the ground. My hair is brown and I have pale skin. I'm around 18 years old, attractive and fashionably plump—an upper class girl ripe for the pickin'. (Eerily, I would have given myself the same description at that age in this lifetime— only plump wasn't fashionable in the 1970s...)

I look up to see my aunt walking toward me. I smile warmly and am happy to see her. We're very close and I love her more like a sister than an aunt. She had arranged for us to meet so we could talk. As soon as she sits down I sense the gravity in her mood. It's serious.

"Dear, we know what you've been doing and your father is sending him away." I immediately know what she's talking about and turn a shade of sick white as the blood drains from my rosy cheeks and terror replaces the happiness I'd had just moments ago.

The scene flashes to him and me in the barn. We're making passionate love surrounded by piles of hay, unaware of anything but each other and the intensity of our sweaty bodies moving in unison.

"Him" is the slave I have fallen in love with. He's tall, with long slender arms and dark brown skin. He has cracked my heart wide open and freed my spirit from the shackles of my traditional upbringing.

The scene jumps to me hanging clothes on the line in our sprawling back yard. Something causes me to look out to the edge of the property where the trees meet the grass. As I gaze into the woods, desperate grief washes over me, weakening my entire body to the point of almost collapsing in a heap of sadness. I wonder if he'll ever come back. *Why hasn't he come back...?* Just then I hear someone yelling for me from the porch. It's my husband saying that it's time to go. We have children together. Minutes later the family is getting into a carriage that's big enough to hold all of us. Life with this man is something I never wanted but my family insisted upon. Going to bed with him every night is a torturous reminder that the man I truly love is gone.

The final scene is me on my death bed surrounded by my grown children who are clearly upset. I, on the other hand, am entirely numb, feeling nothing about my life, my death, or even my children. Over the years, the sadness and longing gave way to pitiful apathy. All of my emotion left with the man who was sent away and never returned. I became nothing but a shell, married to someone I didn't love—a white man in upper standing of course. As I take my last breath, my children's weeping becomes louder. I'm now hovering above my body watching them grieve from above. It's all over now: my desperate life, the marriage I was forced into, and the children that came out of it.

"3-2-1," says Dr. Weiss. "As you bring your awareness back into this room, you'll remember everything that you just experienced."

I was with my sister at this spiritual conference, and as we opened our eyes, we turned to each other and smiled. The hypnosis session felt like it lasted about ten minutes, but Dr. Weiss said that it lasted for nearly an hour! I was shocked by what I had just seen and experienced as it explained so much. It explained my tendency, even as a young girl, to long for men who were out of my reach. It explained the innocent attraction I had to an African-American substitute teacher who came into our fifth grade class a few times. It wasn't sexual at all; it was just an overwhelming desire to be his friend. I was so enchanted by him that one day while in the kitchen with my mother, we had the following conversation: "Mom, do you know what I'd really like for Christmas?" She was good about Christmas. We didn't have much money, but she always figured out a way to give us exactly what we wanted. "Some time with Mr. Bennett, my substitute teacher."

I asked for nothing else, no toys, clothes or records, just an outing with my substitute teacher.

I was sure she would arrange this too, because that's the way my mom rolled. But Christmas came and went and no one said a word about Mr. Bennett. I've thought of this experience a thousand times, yet I'm just now realizing the absurdity of my request. Mr. Bennet triggered a poignant memory within me. I didn't know what that memory was, but somehow he reminded me that I was missing something that I desperately needed to find. And we wonder where our irrational desires come from?

My past-life experience explains why my spirit chose to be born in 1964—exactly three months after the Civil Rights Act was passed. Discrimination had become illegal. Only then was I willing to return to this seemingly God forsaken planet. It gives me the chills to even write about it. I might have come from a family that owned slaves, but I fell in love with one. He wasn't a slave to me; he was a human being. This is a tragic chapter of American history, and I am beyond honored to be alive now when the balance of power is finally shifting.

Lastly, the past life regression explains my irrational fear of abandonment resulting in the tendency to over attach to the men in my life. Once I fell in love with Man #1, I wasn't leaving.

Eventually I would have to, but with all due respect to him now, the insanity of that relationship should have ended within the first year. When my young brother heard the song Addicted to Love by Robert Palmer, he said, "That's you Kim. You're addicted to love." Even my twelve-year-old brother knew that something about this on-again, off-again teenage relationship was irrational.

What was really going on was that I wasn't going to let my lover get away this time, no matter how bad the relationship was. Thankfully I did eventually break away. It was like a drug addict kicking a long-standing heroin habit though—hard as hell. And just because I was able to let him go, it didn't mean that my pattern of fiercely attaching to men was healed... far from it. I simply took my pattern with me and brought it into the next relationship. Learning about my past life, while desperately sad, liberated me. Once I understood why I did what I did, I could start to heal. I no longer feel that past life regressions are irrelevant. They can provide tremendous insight into our current circumstances and the often irrational fears that we have and choices that we make. These memories can act as a door leading to a new, healthier way of being.

The truth is that I entered this life with a piece of my spirit still tethered to my past. In order to be a free spirit, we need to view each life event as a puzzle piece. Each person, place or situation that we are attracted to holds a clue to where our spirit lies. Moving toward an object of attraction is natural, but we can't chase it, consume it or even destroy it to get our spirit back. Our challenge is to move toward whatever or whoever we're attracted to and enjoy it until we begin to feel tension inside, which acts as a signpost telling us to go within, feel our feelings and reclaim the missing puzzle piece of our soul. When the puzzle is complete, we are able to love freely without becoming tangled.

Ch-ch-ch-changes...

Maybe the reason that free spirits are so rare is that doing our own emotional work in the context of a relationship is no fun at all. In fact, it's downright difficult to change a dynamic that's been in place for years, decades or even lifetimes. But when we're honest with ourselves, it's obvious when aspects of our relationships are unhealthy. After moving back to Phoenix, I decided to get my master's degree in counseling so that I'd have the credentials to teach what I had learned. My undergraduate degree was in communication, so these two aspects of my education, along with my commitment to inner peace, created a strong desire for healthy relationships. More importantly, when one's spirit awakens, everything unhealthy automatically gets in line for transformation. Thankfully it doesn't happen all at once. But one by one—starting with the biggest—every single pattern of behavior that chains spiritual freedom comes to light, compelling us to redesign the pattern.

Luckily, I didn't have much to transform with my immediate family, although I did need to stop seeking my father's approval in a ten-year-old sort of way. He worked a lot when I was growing up and I never seemed to get enough of him. Because there was no abuse and he clearly loved me, all that was required were a couple of difficult conversations along with deliberately shifting my behavior from constant approval seeking to simply doing what I know in my heart to be the right thing. Even though this isn't much, untangling from this childish need for approval was still tough. Redesigning long-standing patterns can feel like ripping off a band aid. Sometimes it seems much easier to simply tolerate the low-level discomfort that's been going on for years than to try to relate in a new way. Free spirits tend to have a low tolerance for dysfunction, because even when subtle, it's a drag on one's energy. I've worked with many clients who were untangling from parents. Age is always irrelevant, whether we're in our twenties or sixties, relationship dynamics remain the same until we have had enough and the emotional risk that comes with initiating change becomes preferable to the status quo.

Another reason that changing the rules of a relationship is so hard is because in addition to feeling the tension of transformation, healthy change dislodges all the emotion that's been stuffed while tolerating the dysfunction. The longer the pattern has been in place, the more emotion we collect around it. But once we change our behavior, the pent up emotion, often sadness, anger or resentment, begins to dissipate. My father and I became closer than ever after transforming our outdated dynamic. This man has been a constant source of wisdom and support in my life—a presence for which I am deeply grateful.

Before my past life regression, I figured my relationships with men were mostly based on my yearning for my father's attention. Freudian, I know, but what else is one to think? Now I know better. There may be some truth to picking someone like your mother or father, but there are so many other forces... This is why it's dangerous to "blame" our parents for anything. Sometimes we don't know what else might be compelling us to do what we do. Perhaps it's a steamy mixture of past lives and childhood patterns blended together to form a witches brew that we can't resist even though its dark power keeps us trapped in dysfunction that's lasted a thousand years. Whatever the invisible force is that tries to keep us in chains, breaking free from childish patterns is a prerequisite for feeling free in any relationship. After becoming a grown up with my parents, untangling from others started to get easier. Had I done it sooner, I would have likely saved myself a decade of heartache. My first two relationships required walking away to untangle, but it took a very long time and required every ounce of courage I could muster. The first one took place before my awakening, so I'm cutting myself some slack there. But my relationship with man #2, my former husband, was post awakening. I was shocked at how tangled I became with him. Freeing myself was so hard. It has never been that hard again and I doubt it ever will be. That's the beauty of the Modern Hippie journey—it has momentum. The more of our spirit we recollect along the way, the easier it is to stay true to that spirit.

My ex-husband is now more like a brother/friend. He helps me raise our daughter, but the form of relationship we once had has completely dissolved. I have little or no contact with some of the people that I needed to untangle from and that's okay, because in truth, we are all connected anyway.

I was reminded of this during my break-up with Man #3. Our relationship had its ups and downs and we broke up a couple of times in the first several years we were together, but the last leg of our relationship seemed like it was going to be solid. We'd both committed to doing what we knew we needed to flourish as a couple. We moved into a new house for a fresh start and everything looked promising. But as time passed, it was clear that it wasn't going to work. The day I said out loud that we should go our separate ways, he agreed without any hesitation. It seemed like he was already gone, but forgot to tell me. Meanwhile, I'd spent the last six months trying to get us back on track. After our "talk," I went into my bedroom to try and collect my thoughts. I was deeply sad and confused about what had just transpired. Finally I decided to go for a walk. With just a few steps my energy started to lift. I began talking to God, the way I tend to do, and I heard myself say, "Maybe this isn't such a big deal. Maybe we are just in different places now and in truth we will always be connected." I said, "God, if this is true, show me a sign." And then I thought for a moment what a good sign would be to affirm this truth. I decided on an owl for the wisdom it represents. "God, if this is true, please show me an owl." About ten minutes later I saw people looking up and pointing to a tree. Then I heard, *hoo, hoo.* I looked up and would you believe that a huge owl flew out of the tree and landed on another branch? I swear that owl looked right at me when it landed.

I go on walks almost every day and I have yet to see another owl. Putting Spirit in charge means that we have to be okay with the form of our relationships changing. Change is an inescapable part of life, is it not? All of nature changes form, so why should human beings be exempt? The way I see it, we have two choices: either hold on to what's familiar and comfortable the way I did the first half of my life or put Spirit in charge and fasten your seatbelt. My seatbelt is fastened. As I untangle from one person after another, my spirit recollects back into my body where it belongs, increasing the velocity of its expression and clearing old emotion that would otherwise bog it down. This isn't easy, but I continuously commit to life's agenda, which is always changing and always extending in its own way and on its own time. My growing spirit allows me to flow more like a Modern Hippie and less like a fearful child. I'm also able to process my feelings quicker so that I don't allow the accumulated weight of emotion to throw me off balance. I might allow a heavy emotion to linger for a minute, but that's all it is—a minute. And the second I identify that something is weighing on me, I address it. First, by taking a hard look at myself to make sure I'm being impeccable with my own thoughts and behavior, and second, by looking at the situation from the highest perspective—that of an owl. Finally, I'm honest with whoever else is involved. What I don't do is project my B.S. on to them while they project on to me. All that crap does is get us tangled. Clarity has its perks. It allows you to see when someone else is projecting. Without you projecting in kind, there is no drama and everything is allowed to dissipate. My newfound freedom gives me another choice as well. I don't need to stay around year after year hoping that a person will change. If it becomes clear that a situation isn't healthy, I back up and sometimes disappear like a super-hero.

We are designed to be in relationships. Research shows that those of us who have strong social support are healthier and live longer. We relax and expand in the presence of love. The Modern

Hippie has an open heart, which means that she can love just about anyone. Strangers begin to feel like friends. We are discerning though. We instinctively know who we can dance toward and who we should dance away from. It's subtle, like a light breeze on your skin. Spirit is our guide. Sometimes, however, the guidance doesn't even register in our conscious mind, like a child running toward someone he instinctively trusts and running away from someone unsavory. As long as we maintain a strong connection to our spirit, we will be effortlessly guided toward those with whom we can freely exchange energy. Here we have the free spirit dance—it's ongoing and with multiple partners. Unlike some of our hippie predecessors, most of us don't have multiple sexual partners, as it's clearly a different time, but spirit transcends physical intimacy. We can spiritually dance with an old man walking down the street or a toddler standing next to us in the coffee shop. It's still free love, but resembles compassion more than passion.

Chapter 4

The Voice of Spirit

I haven't seen Roover (my imaginary childhood friend) in quite some time, but I've made some new otherworldly friends. While the mystic in me resonates with the essence of all world religions, my "besties" can be found at the heart of Christianity. I cherish a deep connection with Jesus and the angels. I also like to chat with family and friends on the other side from time to time. My first experience with this happened one evening after going for a run. My vibration was still high from the exercise (having a high vibration is a prerequisite for communicating with the spirit world). I spontaneously asked the angels if I was supposed to channel messages for my clients from their family and friends on the other side. What came to me is that my life's work is not that, but rather to bring down universal spiritual truths and translate them in a way that is easy to understand. This made complete sense, as that is what I've always done, but in the very next breath I said, "Okay then, I'll just speak to my family and friends on the other side." Then I got up from my bed where I was sitting and went in to the living room and, still in contemplation, sat back down on my big rattan rocking chair. I looked up and noticed my beloved grandmother sitting on the worn, gold velvet couch in front of me that used to be in her and my grandfather's home before they passed. It was lovely to see her as we were very close when I was young. We chatted for a moment and she shared her perspective regarding a conflict I was having with a friend at the time. Although she was a spirit, she seemed to have retained her earthly biases. That is, no one should mess with her "perfect" granddaughter. I was surprised that she was aware of what I was going through. My grandfather then appeared, sitting next to her. I looked up and had a thought and the next thing I knew they were gone. Just as I started to feel sad that I got distracted from their presence, I noticed my other set of grandparents sitting there. They had been divorced from each other twice in their lives, and my grandmother remained bitter until the day she died. But here they were together, almost giddy, sitting as close as possible. Good to know they reunited. After they left, my great aunts came through. One of them told me that my ex-husband was not "the one." The other aunt chimed in, "He is sexy though!" This comment was true to her personality as she never married but definitely liked her men. The stream of friends and family members went on for nearly fifteen minutes before I had to shut the invisible door to heaven and say that I was done for the evening. This temporary lifting of the veil was a beautiful affirmation that our loved ones are all still here and aware of what's happening in our lives. And while I cherish their opinions and seek them out from time to time, I mostly refer to my own spirit and God, Jesus and the angels for guidance. It gives me great comfort to know that these spiritual beings have my back. I *never* feel alone. I know we all have our own brand of spirituality and that talking to dead people isn't for everyone. Frankly, I'm even a little surprised that I went in this direction, as I wasn't even able to walk down the hall to go to the bathroom in the middle of the night for several years after watching the movie Sixth Sense. But, like many people, I have had very real experiences that have cemented my faith in the afterlife and my belief that we have abundant spiritual support during our journey here on earth.

In my times of deepest despair I tend to call on Jesus. My beautiful daughter Anna was born two and a half weeks early. She still emerged a healthy 6.7 pounds. When the nurse put her in my arms, my baby stared at me so deeply that I cried. This little being transmitted pure love, looking at me as if she'd known me for a million years. After being released from the hospital, we took her to the doctor for a standard infant check up. The doc noticed some white spots on her throat and was concerned about a growing infection. She instructed us to go straight to the hospital. In a state of shock, we got in the car and drove our tiny new baby to the hospital. That night after everyone left, I was all alone in the cold, dark hospital room with my sick infant. I was terrified. The only thing I could do was call out to Jesus... *Jesus, I need a miracle. Please help my baby...* Right then I felt an unmistakable wave of peace flow through my body, and I knew that Anna would be okay. The next morning we had a visit from the doctor who admitted her. She looked at Anna's throat and said, "Oh, it's much better, look mom!" She gestured for me to look and sure enough the white spots had all but diminished. We still had to stay nine more days as she received medicine through an IV, but in my heart I knew it was just a formality because my baby girl was already healed.

I believe that Jesus and other spiritual masters are there for us and want us to ask for help—not just with the big things in our lives but the little things. Angels too. I've had so many amazing experiences with the angels, particularly Archangel Michael who is a protective presence in many of our lives. He loves to give direct advice and offers metaphors to help me to process challenging events. When my relationship with man #3 ended, Michael said, "My dear, it was the last inning of the World Series and he dropped the ball." In other words, it's over. Each of these metaphors feels like a liberating burst of clarity. Sometimes I need more than one. He'll give me one and it will help me for a few days, and then I find myself stuck again, so I'll ask for another. Archangel Michael is no-nonsense. Sometimes I can feel the wrath of his sword slice out something in my life that would otherwise diminish my spirit. He's also very funny. I find all the angels to be funny. Once

I was driving in my car feeling very sorry for myself during a particularly long bout of single-hood. I kept thinking, *why can't I meet anyone...* Then an upbeat song by Babyface came on the radio, "It's a good day...Celebrate love, celebrate life..." I got this vision of the angels dancing like the Temptations! They were rocking side to side, moving their arms in synch with the music. The entire song was choreographed! The message was for me to snap out of it and appreciate all the love in my life. I later taught this dance to my daughter and we performed it at her sixth birthday party in front of the family. In my experience all we need to do is ask for the angels' involvement in our lives if that's what we want. It's like having a spiritual adviser, life coach and best friend all wrapped up in one loving presence.

Karma and Intuition

As my mother used to say, "Kimberly, some people live and learn and others just live." Freedom is dependent upon the ability to learn our life lessons and not repeat the same mistakes over and over again. However, God knows that I'm not above repeating the same un-evolving behavior ad nauseam. I'll get a bright, shiny, clear insight and in the blink of an eye, karma, the energetic momentum of past choices, lures me into unconsciously sliding back into my familiar groove—sort of like sinking into the warn cushion of your couch where any chance of being productive is cancelled out by the remote control. But rather than getting angry at this force that is so good at keeping me stuck, I now welcome karma into my life and view it as an invitation to consciously choose again. I see it as a friend who continuously supports my evolution. I do my very best to use mindfulness to interrupt the momentum of karma with the goal of burning it off completely so that I'm free to create my life in any way that I'd like. Of course, good karma is preferable to bad karma, but my goal is no karma—no energetic residue pulling me in a certain direction.

We know we're burning through karma when life gets progressively easier. Because I came into this life with the pattern of deeply longing for an absent man, I repeated that pattern, choosing men who were out of reach. When I first met man #2, a little voice in my head said, "He's unavailable." When I learned that he was single, I was shocked! But instead of being physically unavailable he was emotionally unavailable, which was just as painful, if not more. But no energetic dance is one-sided. I have to take responsibility for my part, as I was trying to get him to complete me when cultivating wholeness is an inside job. Over the years I've had to learn that my primary relationship is the one I have with myself, and any man that I choose will perfectly mirror the level of love, care and affection that I give to myself. I had to learn this lesson the hard way. Crying tears of grief while asking the universe why I was treated so poorly gets redundant after a while. At a point, the voice of my Angels got louder than my sobs and sternly said, "Take a look in the mirror my dear—they treat you the way you treat you." After having this insight, I started treating myself *really* well and have progressively attracted more loving men, right in line with my own self-love journey.

In addition to applying mindfulness, I now check in with my intuition in the midst of karmic temptations. So when everything in me wants to jump on the back of a motorcycle with a bad boy (yes, I still have the impulses of a sixteen year old...), I take a moment and ask my growing spirit for its opinion. Now, more often than not, my spirit has more power than any lower impulses and quickly redirects me toward evolution and freedom. At the same time, I've had to learn to forgive myself when karma has its way with me.

This happens, and whenever it does, I experience a loss of energy and inner peace. Mostly, it's with simple things, like enjoying that extra glass of wine only to wake up less than refreshed, or saying something rude instead of kind in a moment of frustration. Karma is still present and I can feel its tug. I'm grateful, however, that it's only a tug. Early on it was more like a vortex—I had no power over the momentum of energy that seemed to pull me into various self-sabotaging behaviors.

In the beginning of my journey, unconscious choices fed my existing karma. But once I reintegrated enough of my spirit back into my body, I was able to apply mindfulness to temptations and interrupt this compelling force of momentum. And while I'm getting better every day, lapses in mindfulness will cause me to carelessly leave the door open for karma to stroll back into my life. Sometimes I leave the door ajar when I act from my ego instead of my spirit. The difference is that I'm aware of my mistake right away and can respond more immediately. The way I can tell I've collected a bit of karma is that the situation sticks to me and I continue to think about it. If I can't let something go, it means that I have some clean-up to do.

It just happened the other day during a hot yoga class. I'm in class going through a flow series and my body is raining sweat. The teacher is directing us at a slower pace than usual, which makes it even harder. At one point I move ahead of her directions. She promptly tells the class, "Stay with my words please." Being hot and irritated, I motion with my hand for her to move on! I immediately felt the karmic spillage. I was being intolerant of her teaching style. I mentally justified my behavior for about five minutes and then realized that I needed to clean up my mess. After the torture session was over, I put on dry clothes and then went to find the teacher to thank her as I always do. "I'm sorry for jumping ahead in class," I said.

She promptly replied, "No! It's fine! I hope you didn't feel targeted. You have a beautiful practice." We enjoyed a little spiritual dance as I cleaned up my energetic mess. So many times we put our energy into justifying our behavior rather than looking at ourselves. I've learned that any time my behavior is not aligned with my highest self, I have two choices: either hold on to my judgment about the other person or take responsibility for myself. If I judge too many times, my judgments gain energy, thereby compelling me to repeatedly entertain them.

A free spirit is wholly integrated and flowing without obstruction. Karma is made up of fragmented pieces of energy that take away from the integrated, expressive nature of Spirit. Most of us have karma in many areas of our lives as a result of placing our attention and energy on the ego's justifications, rants and insecurities instead of following Spirit's lead. We unconsciously build our own prison where energy can no longer flow because of all the judgments, justification and pent-up emotion. Eventually we're stuck with a web of entangled thoughts, beliefs, emotions and behaviors that extend beyond us and become tangled with other's karmic patterns. It's messy business, but once we've committed to spiritual freedom, we go about the business of untangling one thought, one word, and one action at a time. We undo our karmic choices more for ourselves than for others. I've found the process of undoing to be divinely orchestrated. If we are serious, Spirit will present us with one opportunity after another to make a better choice—a more mindful choice.

When we get to a certain level of integration and clarity, the effects of karma become immediate. The other day, I had the privilege of having karma knock me on my butt after acting unconsciously. My daughter was taking care of my sister's cat while they were on vacation and had misplaced their house key. It had been a long day and I was frustrated. I told her under no uncertain terms that her behavior was irresponsible while huffing, puffing and audibly sighing. Finally after looking everywhere and making a few calls, she discovered that she'd left the key in her dad's car.

"Fine," I snapped. "Let's go to the grocery store and then pick up the key," We did just that, went and fed the cats and then proceeded home. As we were putting the groceries away, I realized that my purse was missing. I couldn't imagine where it was, but assumed I had left it at my sister's house. I asked Anna to finish with the groceries and then rushed out without a phone, driver's license or anything else I usually have when I grab my purse to leave the house. I checked at my sisters, no purse. I wondered if someone took it while we were in feeding the cats. I decided to head back to the grocery store and see if by chance it was there. I rushed in and asked the manager if anyone turned in a purse. She said, "Is it brown and does it weigh about 100 pounds?"

"Yes!" I exclaimed. I had left my purse in the cart outside—open no less, because I'm very lazy about snapping it shut. A store employee who was collecting carts found it and handed it in to the manager. Right after profusely thanking the store manager and the young man who found it, I said a grateful prayer and called Anna. I apologized for being so impatient and unkind. I told her that the incident gave me a forceful reminder that everyone forgets things from time to time and that there was no reason for me to be so rude. "Thanks Momma," is all she said, without any hint of attitude or resentment.

I had to ask myself, "Who's teaching who here?"

Here Comes the Sun

One of the benefits of taking ultimate responsibility for our thoughts and actions is that as the clouds of karma begin to dissipate, intuition is able to shine through. Intuition is what's left when karma is burned off. *Instead of falling into the momentum of the past, we begin to heed the voice of the present.* I was always intuitive—I could sense things—but I often ignored it or talked myself out of it. But now that I've recollected my spirit, its voice is very loud. Luckily, we're all starting to claim our intuition. I heard Carolyn Myss speak the other day. In her matter of fact, don't-give- me-any-shit manner, she said that we are all intuitive beings and it's high time we incorporate the sixth sense into our lives as naturally as we use our other senses. I couldn't agree more. As long as we view intuition as a gift that is only bestowed upon "special ones," we ignore the built-in radar that allows us to navigate life consciously. Free spirits depend on the ability to flow in and out of harm's way without catching any toxicity or getting tangled up with lower energies.

At the college where I teach, students explore their preferred learning style. Some are visual, whereas others are auditory or kinesthetically inclined. And I've noticed that our preferred way of receiving intuition is usually in line with whatever sense we use most to process information in the world. I once told a highly clairvoyant friend that I needed to open my third eye so that I could see more intuitive pictures. She said, "Why? You experience direct knowing," as she gestured pulling energy directly into the top of her head. "That's even more direct insight!" she exclaimed. The point is, we all have different ways of processing information—intuitive or otherwise. I'm not visual in life and, except on rare occasions, I don't receive intuitive pictures either. I'm a thinker, so I receive flashes of insight. And I'm an auditory learner who loves to listen to lectures and hear people speak, the intuitive counterpart to this is clairaudience—hearing my inner spiritual voice. It tells me things, like "He's unavailable..." I think it's important to know our preferred intuitive style the same way we know our preferred learning style. Those who are visual are more inclined to be clairvoyant. Those who are kinesthetic or physically oriented are more likely to be clairsentient, getting gut feelings or messages in their bodies. Most of us have access to all of these with one style that is preferred.

All receptors are good. We just need to be careful not to discount any information we receive intuitively. I keep learning the same lesson; when I feel something, I'm right. I've been pretty dense with this one. I want to give everyone the benefit of the doubt and an opportunity to evolve. I want to express myself, talk things through and hear the other person's perspective. But my experience is that people sugar coat, side step or soften their position when they're talking about it. So I've had to learn to trust myself and not be talked out of my intuitive hunches. I love the lesson that Oprah learned from Maya Angelou: when people show you who they are, believe them... the first time. Wow! I could have saved myself a lot of time had I learned that early on. More often than not, people don't tell us who they are, they show us. The more of our spirit we've recollected, the clearer we can see, feel and hear information about who's in front of us. As far as intimate partners go, if a man isn't already evolved to the point of being my equal, a relationship is not in the cards. This wasn't always the case. I would give a lover opportunity after opportunity to choose again and more often than not, karma prevailed. My life's work is to elevate others, but when it comes to an intimate partner, he has to know how to elevate himself or he cannot be with me. I've had to come to terms with the fact that just as there are levels of self (spiritual, emotional, mental, physical), there are levels of Truth.

On a spiritual level, we are all equal and connected, but as human beings, there are emotional, mental and physical levels of truth as well. I'm not going to be with someone who's emotionally undisciplined any more than I would be with someone who's an active drug addict. The spiritual truth that we are all one does not override these other factors while we're still living here on this planet in physical bodies.

When I was younger, I believed that it was "spiritual" to allow people in and give them chance after chance. I somehow thought that's what it meant to forgive. I no longer believe that. Sometimes we have to let go of a relationship in order to forgive. My experience has been that when I spend energy trying to elevate another, my own journey up the mountain is delayed. Instead of ascending, I zigzag trying to get my partner to ascend with me. Moving on is not selfish. The higher we get, the more we inspire others to come along.

I work on every level of myself, and expect the people in my inner circle to do the same. I tend to my spirit through daily meditation and mindfulness. I stay emotionally clear by being honest and processing my feelings as they occur. These days, I'm pretty clear emotionally, but for the first decade of this journey, I had to process ancient emotions that were hibernating within me. Feeling and releasing old emotions was grueling, but had to be done, as everything unprocessed accrues karma. The Modern Hippie does not tiptoe around her emotional landmines. Instead, she actively looks for them and excavates them so she can dance freely, knowing that she's cleared the land beneath her and no longer has to worry about tripping over live wires. This emotional clarity also means that no one can push her hot buttons because they are no longer there. On the mental level, I strive to keep my thoughts positive and productive. This has also taken years of discipline, as my thoughts used to run me like a wild animal. I've had to tame this animal and show it who's in charge.

Not only does my daily practice involve mental discipline through mindfulness, I honor my body physically by paying attention to what it needs for balance. This way, my spirit can flow through it like a fresh river and not run into pollution that might inhibit or clog its expression. Complete integration of spirit into one's mind and body requires a deep commitment to ongoing growth. It's difficult for me not to observe and intuitively perceive the level of spiritual integration in others. First off, it's my job. As a counselor and energy coach, I use my intuition to help people identify and transform the patterns that cause them to lose energy and delay their evolution. I'm not able to simply turn this off when I'm not working. Without judgment, I allow myself to perceive the truth about others. For example, someone I meet might have pure intentions and a good heart but be so tangled up with family drama that she is emotionally drained. Most often I keep these insights to myself unless I'm asked or working with a client. But I do use this information to guide my choices about who to spend time with. Isn't that what intuition is for? To guide us effortlessly toward our highest life? By being this honest with myself, I'm able to actually love others more. I accept them for who they are and where they are without needing to change them. By honoring me, I honor them, knowing that we are all headed in the same direction.

Dreams, Water and Signs

I've been getting more and more intuitive information in my dreams and sleep. The other day I dreamt that a friend of mine was grieving. In the dream I was hugging her and helping her process her grief. Later I found out that her brother passed away suddenly from a heart attack. I've learned to pay attention to my dreams and the information they provide. Sometimes I'll wake up in the middle of the night after receiving a big intuitive message about a situation I'm grappling with at the time. I've learned that all I have to do is ask the question and the answer will come. If I'm not able to receive it during the day, it will bubble up at night when my mind is open and receptive.

Some people regularly receive insights and answers to their questions in the shower. Water seems to be a powerful conduit through which intuitive information flows and is amplified.

Signs and synchronicity in the outside world also provide intuitive guidance. Everything can be viewed as information to the refined eye. We each have our own intuitive language. Signs and symbols mean different things to different people. Spirit uses the symbols that make sense to us. Bubbles have appeared to me when I've needed to lighten up. Once, when I was sitting in my car at a red light on my way to the park to collect my thoughts after an upsetting fight with Man #3, I noticed a bubble floating in front of my windshield. I started looking around and saw hundreds of bubbles all around my car and up into the sky. There were no children around or any source at all. They simply surrounded me with bubble love, helping me to shift my focus to the bigger picture.

Another time, in the middle of summer in Arizona when the temperature was well over 110, Anna and I walked out of a movie theater to be greeted by a single bubble. It floated in front of us and captured our attention, moving up and down as if dancing. At one point, it even touched the scorching hot asphalt and didn't pop! We laughed in amazement and proceeded to our car. When we arrived, we noticed that the front tire was flat. "Oh well," we said, knowing full well that the bubble had been a light-hearted reminder to stay cool.

I don't think it matters if we believe in God, angels, Jesus or another religious figure, or if we look to nature as our source of inspiration. What matters is that we believe in the divine intelligence that permeates all of life. This life is consciousness itself and makes everything so much better if we let it. I can't imagine my life without the huge presence (and presents) of Spirit. It's my ground, my vision, my support, my wisdom and my inspiration. I am so grateful that I've built my house on this unmovable stone. It gives me the strength I need to live my highest and most loving life. Everything could crumble and I would still have my spirit.

Chapter 5

Finding Your Free Weight

When I first figured out that feeling happy and free inside was going to require me to go with life's flow instead of my own, cleaning up my diet was the last thing on my mind. Sure, I needed to stop obsessing about food, giving myself guilt trips, and hijacking bakeries, but once I got that under control, food issues became more of a side dish while my plate became full with the emotional/mental side of transformation.

However, as I moved closer to becoming a Modern Hippie, the desire to feel completely free and at peace in my own skin grew. The concept of *free weight* came to me: The weight at which one is completely comfortable in her own skin. The desire to find my free weight reignited the physical part of my journey, the part that brings me back to the place where I started so many years ago. But the self-conscious chubby girl is slowly giving way to a body-confident free spirit. I share the physical part of my journey here, starting with the early changes that allowed me to get my runaway eating under control so that I could focus on the spiritual psychotherapy taking place as I completed the workbook from *A Course in Miracles*. And I share the more recent revelations that continue to move me toward physical freedom. My hope is that you will resonate with something in this chapter that will help you on your own journey toward freedom.

Does Skinny Buy Peace?

Aside from being a toddler and the summer after my milkshake diet, the thinnest I've ever been was one semester in college when I had the privilege of attending two psychology classes back-to-back with a professor on whom I harbored a mad crush. The classes were held in an auditorium with stadium style seating, and I made sure to arrive early to get a seat in the front row so that no one could block my view of him putting his finger up to his mouth as he pondered Freud's theories or the social nature of crime. Perhaps the uninterrupted wave of infatuation dulled my appetite, but for whatever reason, I didn't eat during the day that semester and ended up dropping fifteen pounds off my normally doughy body. I was shocked to find out that my level of inner peace didn't rise to the height of Mount Everest as my weight descended. In fact, not only did my inner peace fail to rise to amazing heights, it didn't rise at all! I may have stopped thinking about food for a minute, but other random and meaningless obsessions immediately moved into the vacant space within my brain. Lesson learned. Skinny does not buy peace. I've also known beautifully curvy women who glide freely though life, loving their bodies without ever giving food a second thought aside from planning and enjoying their next delicious meal. The point is that there is no formula for how to be at peace. We can be a free spirit at any size as long as we are true to ourselves on every level—physical, mental, emotional and spiritual. And if we lose weight, either on purpose or on accident, without addressing the emotions that we were trying to stuff in the first place, our spirit will remain bound.

There is one thing I've discovered about feeling comfortable in my own skin: In order to get to a free and peaceful place physically, we need to be on a path that is free and peaceful. In other words, beating oneself up for being overweight and then feverishly embarking on a deprivation diet simply serves to "feed" the lack of peace within oneself, and regardless of the weight at which one arrives, it will not be our free weight. We may have shed the extra fat, but we will not have learned to be at peace. We have so much to untangle from here. There is a collective pull toward body image obsession that is so strong it can grip even the most comfortable woman. I am speaking for women here and I am speaking for myself, because while I'm at peace in my own skin 80% of the time, I still slip into body neurosis more often than I'd like. Feeling less than my best can almost always be traced to a bout of mindless eating. You may be able to relate to this; if I'm making conscious choices and being mindful during every meal, there's not much that can shake my feelings of physical well-being and the sense that I'm at least headed in the right direction. On the other hand, if I lack mindfulness in my eating choices for too long, my behavior leads me down a path of self-doubt.

Whenever I find myself headed down the wrong path, I remind myself that this mindless behavior has created momentum that needs to be reversed. I try to catch myself, change my behavior and close this peace gap as quickly as possible because my desire isn't to be a partial free spirit, but to be wholly free, both for myself and for everyone one of us who has ever grappled with body image issues.

Gratitude for being substantially liberated is in order because the pain of being completely tied up in body neurosis was nearly unbearable for me as a young woman. It seemed that I never had a peaceful moment in my own head. Now, all that stands between me and 100% freedom are the faint remnants of those old negative thoughts and whatever is left of the ancient emotions that I chose to stuff with each bite of food, not my lovely, healthy and somewhat curvy body.

Fat doesn't bind everyone's spirit, but for me, the little padded cells (fat cells, not prison cells, although eerily similar) that comforted and protected me as a child eventually turned into a form of spiritual imprisonment. This is because my particular brand of fat was emotional fat. Emotional fat accumulates from devouring food in order to unconsciously ease feelings of angst—a sure way for one's spirit to get buried under layers of sticky fat and emotion resembling that of a fat casserole.

Knowing that emotion is simply energy (spirit) in motion, I've come to the conclusion that emotional eating is a form of spirit stuffing. Clearly, the temporary avoidance of negative feelings is not a good idea. The emotion that we're trying to avoid just gets locked in place until we finally decide to allow it to do its thing and move on through our body. Only at that point, we need to release the fat along with the emotion—double whammy. Unfortunately, the only reasonable antidote for this malady is another meal... Eventually we find ourselves simultaneously running from the emotion that threatens to overwhelm us while running toward the next meal—a vicious cycle to be sure. Releasing emotional fat is like asking a child to get rid of the stuffed animal he's slept with since he was a baby, but if we avoid our own transformation for too long, the pent-up energy will erupt in the form of sickness or an emotional breakdown.

Regular fat is not as daunting. My friend Angie loves her sweets. Give her a piece of cake and she's in hog heaven. She was thin most of her life and just recently put on some weight due to a slowing metabolism and her sheer enjoyment of decadent treats. Angie's fat is happy fat. With or without the extra weight, she's a free spirit. It is emotional fat that binds the spirit, not the kind that comes from enjoying food and forgetting that your metabolism isn't what it was twenty years ago. Losing happy fat is way different from losing emotional fat. Happy fat is, well, untangled—pretty straight forward. Cut out soda and add a little exercise and BAM, off melts ten pounds. But losing emotional fat is *so* different. No one wants to experience old emotion leaving the body and hunger pangs at the same time! So we continue to abandon ourselves and mindlessly shove food into our mouths, temporarily escaping our angst while unwittingly creating more—all the while telling ourselves that it would feel so good to just lose the weight. And it would, but not for the reasons that we think. Yeah, it's great to fit into your favorite pair of jeans, and the compliments are nice too, but the real liberation comes from a freely flowing spirit. When we finally get the courage to face our feelings and embrace the initial discomfort of eating less, each pound of emotional fat that is lost is a piece of spirit found. This is why shedding some weight often reveals a less inhibited, more energetic self.

I've found that the hardest part of reversing the emotional eating cycle is just making the decision to do so. Before making the decision to change, we experience a sort of unreasonable, low level terror. It's almost as if the fat cells are screaming, "Wait, let me live! Don't shrink me! I'm human too!" And in a way it's true. These little cells are comprised of life energy just like everything else in the world. It's just that some of our spirit is trapped within them, and if we are to thrive as a whole person, we need to let everything go that imprisons our spirit. So we move forward like brave soldiers and do what we need to do for the good of the whole. We thank our emotional fat for all of the extra padding and comfort we've received over the years and tell these little cells that it's time to "let go and let God."

You may have escaped the body image hell that so many of us have fallen into, and if so, bless your heart and skip to the next chapter. But for the rest of us, what better time is there to face our fears and let Spirit direct us toward right action? Perhaps we're guided to have a smoothie instead of a bagel for breakfast; endure a little hunger instead of snacking on chips; take our butts out for a walk rather than veg out in front of the TV. With Spirit's support, we find that we have the courage to withstand the symptoms of cellular transformation: irritability, boredom, doubt, frustration and often grief or sadness that's been buried for a very long time. We feel our feelings, process them and finally release them along with the fat that's been weighing us down. Little by little we begin to feel lighter in our body and soul, and over time, actually lose the desire to impede our free flowing spirit with a bucket of carbs. Our renewed spirit continues to subtly direct and encourage us toward our free weight by feeding us what we're truly hungry for: life energy.

All this is done gently and peacefully, despite occasional moments of discomfort. We are kind toward ourselves with the knowledge that self-discipline is a form of self-love, a temporary requirement that enables us to get out of our own way so that Spirit can move in and form a bridge to inspiration—a land where we eat well because it feels good, not because we have to force ourselves to do so. In the meantime, we remember that a mistake is just that, a mistake, not a permanent scarlet letter to remind us of our inherent shame and utter lack of self-discipline.

As the voice of the ego recedes into the background, we are comforted by the fact that as a blossoming free spirit, we don't require or desire perfection, only to be comfortable in our own skin. Any weight that hinders our spirit needs to go, but beyond that, a little junk in the trunk is a non-issue, even something to be proud of, thanks to the likes of Jennifer Lopez and Beyonce. Society desperately needs more of us to become fully liberated from body neurosis so that the template of body love, body peace, and body freedom are more readily accessible in the collective consciousness. These movements are always contagious, as we wouldn't even have the hippie archetype to pull from if it weren't for the rapid expansion of this movement in the '60s, which left a permanent imprint on our collective mind. Each woman liberated from body image issues makes it easier for the next one to follow in her footsteps. We can sense when a woman is 100% at peace with her body, and interestingly enough, regardless of how big, small, tall or short she is, the spirit that's able to flow through her peaceful being allows her to emanate striking body confidence and an enviable glow. When a woman appreciates herself, we appreciate her. And the opposite is true as well. We can sense when a woman rejects her body, and we automatically inherit the marginalized view that she has of herself.

If the road to one's free weight is paved with peace, then how do we get there? How is it possible to feel at peace at 15, 50 or even 100 pounds over one's "ideal" weight? Inner peace arises from the flow of spiritual energy through one's heart, mind and body. Even before our spirit is fully untangled from food, we can experience increased spiritual flow by acting in alignment with our highest self. When we know that we should be doing one thing, yet we fail to honor ourselves and do something else, we trade integration (integrity) for fragmentation and lose flow. Therefore, regardless of the number that appears on the scale (if you choose to own one of these devious little machines), honoring oneself in the moment is the only way to experience inner peace and to ultimately arrive at one's free weight.

Let's be perfectly clear—honoring oneself is not the same as honoring the ego, which demands rigid behavior without ever delivering the elusive inner peace carrot. And one's free weight is not the number that the ego comes up with that reflects society's ridiculous tendency to make supermodels the gold standard. Sometimes honoring oneself involves enjoying a creamy bowl of double chocolate ice cream (or in my case, a cheesy enchilada), and sometimes it involves having just a little bit or none at all. Most importantly, we honor ourselves by mindfully tuning into our bodies with every slow, delicious bite of whatever it is we choose to eat. With this level of awareness, the one bite that goes beyond the body's optimal balance will be the last. With this level of awareness, the food choice that doesn't lead to inner peace may never see your stomach. We learn to walk the fine line of sensual enjoyment that sits between deprivation and over-consumption. It is not so much about what we eat as how we eat and not so much about the outcome but the process, which ultimately leads to feeling peaceful, confident and free.

Often, we don't even know our free weight until one day we wake up so comfortable in our own skin that it doesn't occur to us that we're any-thing other than a precious, perfect and simultane-ously imperfect version of our self. We have expe-rienced mental and physical peace so many days in a row that our spirit has effectively moved from fragmentation to wholeness and is abundantly flowing. I'm excited to one day see you and shake your hand or give you a hug and enjoy a silent exchange of acknowledgment celebrating that we are both free and at peace in our own skin.

As humans, we will veer from the fine line of balance from time to time, but as you will see from my story, guilt only keeps us repeating the very behavior that we're trying to change. Immediate self-forgiveness is the only way to break free of guilt's grip and get back on track. Denying the importance of food's role in creating a sense of well-being is equally as destructive as a guilt trip though. I've noticed that when I neglect to apply mindfulness to my eating for too many meals in a row, the voice of imbalance starts to override the innate wisdom of my body. All of a sudden, the carb craver keeps screaming for carbs or the inner boozer wants to keep on boozing. Regardless of the imbalance, when it's given too much energy—when we indulge one too many times—it takes on a life of its own. I attribute my 80% liberation to being able to step in at this point and apply my will toward doing what I need to do to get back on track. When the ratio was reversed and I had only 20% body peace and 80% body conflict, I had no idea how to regain my power, much less direct it with my will.

I once heard a clear message from Spirit:

> *You must apply your will over that which you have control.*

This short message may not seem like much at first glance, but really it's a profound statement of truth. We may not have the willpower to immediately shift from eating a bag of cookies to munching on carrots and celery, but perhaps we're able to summon enough power to put down the bag of cookies. Putting down the bag allows some energy to recollect in our solar plexus (center of will). Each choice we make that honors our physical well-being, regardless of how small, increases the amount of energy contained in our center. Over time, this energy culminates into power, and the accumulated power eventually turns into spiritual flow, which is exactly the point at which willpower is replaced by pure inspiration to eat well. The nourishment that comes from good energy flow feels too good to give up, even for junk food...

Sometimes we need a plan until inspiration kicks in, and it's tempting to look everywhere but within for a diet or prescription that will magically unveil our perfect body and therefore perfect life. I've created a few guidelines that work for me and might work for you, but how do you know which plan to follow? *Everybody is different!* We have different histories, sensitivities, preferences, etc. Only the wisdom in your body can tell you what it needs. There's so much great information out there, but we don't know what path works for us unless our spirit provides that feeling of conviction or light-hearted optimism that says, "Give it a try!" Regardless of the path chosen, one thing is certain: struggle and peace cannot co-exist; therefore, any diet that's a struggle won't lead to peace. Nor will it lead to one's free weight, because inner peace is a prerequisite for freedom. My experience is that there are specific behaviors that help one to maintain balance but they are rarely bundled into one diet or eating plan unless you create it yourself. It's usually more like a buffet where we pick and choose what works for us at any given time.

Do One Thing

At the beginning of my spiritual journey when I was still vacillating between desperate guilt from binge eating and ego-driven determination to never do it again, all I wanted was to get out of the hell I'd created and find lasting peace. I needed to somehow regain control and get back in touch with my inner wisdom and guidance. With help from a friend at work, I decided to do a 3-day fast. It was so hard, but because we were doing it together, I was able to stick with it. I didn't lose much weight, maybe a pound or two, but those three days enabled me to take a piece of my power back from the food that owned me. My soul was no longer my own and I needed to do something drastic to get it back. This was the beginning of a long journey that resulted in the bulk of my body neurosis (and fat) melting away as I simultaneously got back in touch with my body's inner wisdom.

If we heed Spirit's directive: *Apply your will over that which you have control,* the one thing that we need to do to begin recollecting our power becomes obvious. Fasting for three days was nothing short of a miracle, but it's what I was guided to do at that time. The "one thing" could have just as easily been quite small. The one thing that begins to reverse the momentum in favor of well-being is different for everyone and changes as we change. I only fully fasted for three days that one time, but what keeps me walking the line between deprivation and over consumption is a regular but mild variation of that original fast. These days, the "one thing" that helps me to maintain balance, inner peace, and ultimately my free weight is one light detox day a week. This involves drinking lemon water or green juice during the day and then having a healthy dinner at night. Several years ago, I found it important to fast all day, but that doesn't work for me now. I typically do my detox on Mondays to set the tone for the week. This light Monday detox allows me to ground my energy which often fragments a little throughout the week and weekend. This also gives my body a chance to release built up toxins, thereby reducing cravings for junk food. And there's now research on the anti-inflammatory benefits of temporarily reducing food intake, known as intermittent fasting or IF. My weekly 18-20 hour fast allows me to mindfully eat whatever I want the rest of the week with the intention of maintaining the quality of my energy. I just happen to want good, healthy food most of the time. If I skip my Monday detox too many weeks in a row (which sometimes I do because no matter how many years I've known that this works for me, I can still get off track when I go on vacation or change my schedule…), I lose peace and gain weight. My liberation can revert to imprisonment in a skinny minute. But this is simply what works for me at this stage of my life. It does so because I have a body type that holds on to stuff (fat, emotions, etc.) and abstaining from food for a little while gives my heart, mind and body an opportunity to release all that has accumulated during the week. For someone like my sister who's lucky enough to have a super charged metabolism, a weekly detox would probably just make her hungry and angry—what my daughter calls "hangry."

What's your one thing? What's the one thing that you know would give you more physical balance right now, but you haven't mustered up the will to do it quite yet? I've found that doing the "one thing" often leads to other things, but if we try to sidestep the one thing that our own spirit is directing us to do, nothing else will work. Perhaps the "one thing" that you intuitively know you need to do is stop drinking soda, yet because this would be so difficult, you decide to exercise more to offset the calories. Exercise is necessary for all of us, but organic and lasting transformation requires that we listen to our intuition and heed its advice by doing the one thing that it's asking us to do now. In doing so, a door opens up that leads to the highest and best version of ourselves. There is no side-stepping when it comes to transformation, but we—human beings—are the only animal with the learned ability to override our instincts and intuition. We'd much rather do what the latest "expert" suggests than do what we know in our heart is right for us. Our body knows exactly what, when and how much it needs, but instead of being deeply present to our own body and inner wisdom, we ingest society's values about how we should look and what we should eat. One day it's good to eat meat and the next day it's not; one era glorifies skinny women and the next era glorifies curvy women. What's the score? Why in the world would we trade our instincts for these wildly changing ideals? It makes no sense. Later I'll share what I call my Free Spirit Diet, which enables me to feel more like a Modern Hippie and less like a neurotic mess, but ultimately we all need to come up with our own approach to wellness and inner peace.

Goodbye Guilt

That initial 3-day fast was just the beginning. I still needed to address the emotions that I'd been stuffing with food—primarily social anxiety and guilt from making poor choices. Guilt was the toughest emotion to shake. It took me a long time to rid myself of this sticky, slimy monster that I'd allowed into my life. Think about it. Guilt is a heavy and dark. Lighter emotions simply flow through us, but guilt and its brother shame are two of the heaviest emotions that exist. They stick to us like glue and trick us into making choices that lead to more guilt and shame as a way to produce more of this low vibrational energy to feed their existence. As I've shared, my pattern was to eat well for a few days and then some force seemingly outside of my control would drive me to binge on a mountain of carbs followed by a nice, long swim in a deep sea of guilt. My ego would eventually kick in and adamantly swear that I will never binge again! But three days later, I would. Ever experienced this madness? Miraculously, I had an insight that it wasn't the food I was addicted to, but the guilt. This is when my insane relationship with food really began to shift. I made a commitment that even if I overate, I would not indulge in the habit of feeling guilty. This insight was so compelling that I have never allowed the darkness of guilt to suck me in ever again. I'm sure if I did something seriously wrong, I would experience guilt and shame, as I'm not a psychopath, but murdering and stealing wasn't my issue; it was merely overeating. Don't get me wrong, every time I ate too much, this greenish, brownish slime would stand at my feet waiting for me to feel guilty so it could regain its power and once again bring me down, but I ignored it and refused. The strangest thing happened. As the guilt within me began to dissipate, the binge sessions became less and less frequent and eventually stopped altogether. This counter-intuitive behavior of releasing guilt even when I overate ended up being the catalyst that allowed my relationship with food to transform. I could have read a thousand diet books and never found the exact ingredient that was required to set myself free. Only by listening to my intuition was I able to pinpoint guilt as the emotion that kept my conflicting behavior in place.

After abolishing guilt from my psyche, I still wasn't sure when or how to eat, as I'd lost complete touch with my own instincts. About this time I began to view my appetite as a friend rather than an enemy, seeing hunger as a sign that the furnace is stoked and ready to burn calories. Eating only when hungry was revolutionary for me. A healthy relationship with my body was finally starting to form. The more I listened and respected my body, the more I was able to relax and move toward my free weight.

After I let go of the guilt and actually started listening to my body, I figured that I might as well go a step further and make choices that would bring me peace. This took me to yet another level of liberation. I would routinely ask myself, "Is eating _____ going to bring me peace?" Sometimes the answer would be "yes" and sometimes the answer would be "no." I listened most of the time because I was not willing to give up my newfound peace and the growing momentum of my flowing spirit.

This is a lifelong journey. As I've mentioned, I haven't always been consistent with my regular detox, but this has gotten better in recent years. The payoff is too compelling to forget. The clearer I feel physically the freer I feel spiritually. Skipping days of drinking coffee, wine, eating sugar, etc. cleans me out and helps prevent toxins from accumulating and emotions from sticking. The cleaner the inner corridors of my body, the easier life energy can flow. I have to be a little flexible and dynamic with my eating though because being super rigid or strict only triggers my past neurosis. I try not to rule out anything completely, but instead, allow myself to go through phases of eliminating certain foods while always trying to minimize exposure to chemicals and added hormones. It's a process and we have to start from where we are. Every person that I talk to is aware of something that they'd like to either give up or add to their diet. Eating for peace involves following your own instincts, as only you know for sure what changes will elevate your diet.

Free Spirit Diet

More recently I have begun to focus on raising my vibration by eating higher vibrational foods.

This is the basis for the Free Spirit Diet, although it's really not a "diet," but an approach to eating that has helped me gradually increase my physical vibration and spiritual capacity. We literally are what we eat. Eating low vibrational foods (old, processed, chemical laden) brings down our physical vibration and spiritual flow. These low vibrating foods require more energy to digest than they provide in the form of nourishment and vitality. We've all experienced how certain foods weigh us down, dampen our mood and siphon our spirit— the opposite of what we're going for here... So as an aspiring free spirit who is becoming more in tune with my body, I naturally gravitate toward a higher vibrational diet (whole, fresh food). The higher we are able to raise our vibration through clean eating, positive thinking and right action, the easier it is to be a raging river of spiritual energy and experience true freedom. The most freeing thing about eating a high vibrational diet is that the desire to eat junk food diminishes because we know it will bring down our vibe! We all have a vibrational set-point, just as we have a weight set-point, and there are specific things we can do to raise our vibrational set point and increase the velocity of spirit moving through us. Raising one's vibrational set-point takes time and consistency.

Just as with relationships and everything else in life, when our vibration elevates above that which surrounds us, we lose interest. Trust me, I never thought that pastries would lose their appeal, but eating one would bring down my vibe so much that aside from enjoying an occasional bite of one of these gooey treats, I pretty much steer clear.

One's energy vibration needs to rise gradually in order for it to sustain at the new level, so I introduce higher vibrational foods a little at a time. This gradual approach also allows me to side-step the ego, which would keep me tangled and tormented forever if it could. Every time I try to quickly and radically change my diet, I run straight into a wall of self-sabotage, so I basically decided to slowly elevate my diet in order to stay out of my ego's radar. Your intuition will reveal the perfect Free Spirit Diet for you, but this is what works for me and some of it may resonate with you.

> **Reset** - Eat extremely clean or fast for one day a week, eliminating sugar, caffeine, alcohol, dairy and gluten. Instead, focus on fresh fruits and vegetables, soups and smoothies. This gives the body a chance to release toxins and loosen emotional attachments to certain foods and drinks.

Reintegrate - After the reset phase, deliberately increase the amounts of fresh fruits and vegetables consumed. Instead of trying to eat less (which tends to only work in the short-term), allow yourself to eat whatever you want, with an emphasis in the healthy stuff. Psychologically, we want to chew the same amount as before, so loading up on fresh fruits and vegetables helps eliminate feelings of deprivation.

Reinvent – Modify your favorite recipes by replacing unhealthy ingredients with healthier options. This way you're able to still enjoy "comfort food" while consuming fewer calories and unhealthy ingredients.

Release -We naturally release toxins through the breath, skin (sweating) and regular elimination. Do whatever you can to assist your body with detox through regular exercise, ideally breaking a sweat, and breathing exercises that involve deep inhalations and exhalations. It also helps to drink lots of water and take a fiber supplement to support regular elimination.

I have found this way of eating to be organic and realistic—the opposite of strict dieting. As we slowly increase our physical vibration, we lose interest in lower vibrating foods. Increased spiritual flow provides the inspiration to stay on track. Transgressions aren't a big deal. You realize you don't feel as good when it happens and get back on track. Eating healthy most of the time is like riding a bike. The moment I start to feel like I'm losing my balance, I make an adjustment and keep on riding.

Adding a healthy dose of mindfulness elevates the *process* of eating and raises the vibration of the food even more. Have you noticed that consciously enjoying a meal results in getting full sooner? I certainly have. If I savor a meal by eating slowly and really tasting every bite, I become satiated way sooner than if I eat quickly, shoving food in my mouth while doing something else. Mindful eating adds spiritual nourishment to our food, allowing us to go beyond full to fulfilled. Slowing down at the dinner table is also good for us physically. As one of my yoga teachers reminded us in class recently, you're supposed to chew your drink and drink your food. In other words, keep whatever you're consuming in your mouth long enough for saliva to initiate digestion. Granted, if we all ate like that, there wouldn't be enough time in the day to overeat!

Ultimately, a high vibrational diet infused with mindfulness allows us to gradually and naturally move toward our free weight—the weight at which we feel most like a free spirit. But ironically, we don't feel like a free spirit because of how much we weigh; we are free because we've chosen to cultivate freedom with every bite.

I once asked God what he thought of the sweet roll of fat protruding from my belly. "I think it's symbolic of your desire to find me," I heard. His words flowed through me on a wave of love, leaving ripples of self-acceptance. Through the eyes of God, I was finally able to see my childhood fat as the culmination of many innocent attempts to find my own spirit.

Nourishment comes in many forms and food is just one. Eating is a sacred ritual for the Modern Hippie who so fully embodies her own spirit. We relish in the various textures, tastes and smells before us as we enjoy a sort of instinctive relationship with this concrete form of energy. Eating is no longer a heady experience, but rather becomes the domain of the gut... just as it should be.

Chapter 6

A New Era

While my life was transforming, likely, so has yours. Our identities have been shifting from ego to spirit, to the point that we are now living in a different world. We are looking at everything—our relationships, jobs, and ourselves—with a different set of eyes. Whereas we used to clench our fists, fearfully holding on to our identity, opinions and possessions, we now gladly release all of that in favor of a free flowing spirit. And with Spirit moving in the direction that was intended (inside out instead of outside in), all that is fear based is being flushed out and we are becoming increasingly clear. *It is impossible to remain defended and open at the same time.* This new way of life is the opposite of how we were living when our energy was being funneled toward preserving our fragile, ego-based identity. It's not that we were ego maniacs, it's just that no one ever taught us that we are so much more than the superficial persona that we believed ourselves to be. As we surrender to the fresh life energy that seeks to flow through us, every aspect of ourselves transforms in order to accommodate Spirit's agenda, which is unobstructed expression. Like our hippie predecessors, this new breed of free spirits is ushering in a new era—the era of transparency—where we see with clear vision and allow ourselves to be seen, having no agenda other than remaining clear and untangled enough to hold on to our newfound spiritual freedom.

Being completely different, we are required to interact with the world in a new way. The old way of relating to our environment no longer works, as the ego-driven world is based on consumption rather than expression, and if we try to play by its rules, we will constrict and starve ourselves of the spirit that is feeding us.

Because I'm slotted with the awesome job of being an interpreter of Spirit, I have been given a new set of rules to navigate this new era. Spirit often speaks in metaphors and this is no exception. The metaphor for living as a Modern Hippie is surfing. Instead of chasing spirit, we get to ride its wave. Sound fun? Trying to live by the old rules is going to feel like being stuck in a whirlpool filled with debris—forever moving in circles but never getting anywhere. Instead, we get to ride a wave that has its own momentum, with our hair blowing in the wind, sporting a huge smile. Change of this magnitude occurs gradually and then becomes rapidly contagious; therefore, the more of us who learn to spirit surf, the easier it will be for others to do the same.

Here we go: The seven rules of spirit surfing. Grab your board and prepare to ride the wave of exhilaration that awaits you.

Rule #1: Receive

Prior to the era of transparency, many of us were chasing spirit. We chased it in lovers and at work. We searched for it at the mall, the car dealership and in the plastic surgeon's office. We thought that if we could just get that next thing, we would feel complete. It never worked; the chase was endless. This new era began the moment we slowed down, turned around and looked within. "Aha! There it is. It's been right here all the time. I think I'll take a moment and receive the love that I am." Then we became hooked. Many of us became regular meditators and started seizing every opportunity to be still and know that Spirit is closer than our next breath. Even closer still. Heightened awareness and profound appreciation began to replace the obsessive chase that once characterized our lives. Receiving your spirit is getting on the wave.

I first realized that I was swimming against the natural current instead of surfing spirit when I woke up from my unconscious slumber at the age of 27. I wondered why no one had taught me how to align with this powerful force called life. I still wonder about all of the kids (and adults) who have no idea that just as there are laws of physics, there are laws of spirit. The daily practice of receiving my spirit changed everything for me. I receive my spirit through meditation. I never went through extensive training, but I did attend one meeting in Chicago where we sat in a circle and meditated. Then recently I went to a week-long training on mantra meditation where I realized that the essence of meditation is the same regardless of how it's practiced. My goal is simply to slip into moments of stillness, and I find that the longer I can remain still, the bigger my wave for that day! However, on some days morning meditation isn't enough to carry me through; so if I perceive my wave getting smaller and smaller (my energy dipping), I take a moment to receive my spirit. I close my eyes and breathe deeply. Sometimes I ask Jesus or the angels for support with one thing or another. But I try to avoid mindlessly driving myself into the ground where I inevitably end up shattered and depleted.

Rule #2: See

With spirit comes vision. What we used to think of as vision was only projection. Inner debris covered the lens of our perception and distorted our ability to see. The bank teller, one's spouse, our child's teacher all became shrouded in our own issues. We assumed we could see these souls clearly, but all we really saw was our own unprocessed emotions and judgments. But as we learned to receive our own spirit, it shined a light on this inner debris and helped us claim it as our own. Spirit then held our hand as we felt our old, buried emotion rise up and move into our heart to be felt one more time before leaving the body in a flutter of grief. Then Spirit rushed in and took the place of the ancient emotion that once imprisoned us. What was projection transformed into vision. Through the eyes of Spirit, we began to see past appearances. Compassion replaced judgment as the pain in others became clearly visible. Sometimes, the same vision that reveals one's light and goodness reveals hurtful truths that sting and bring up painful emotions. Above all, we are now willing to see and to accept whatever emotions accompany our vision. With vision, and acceptance of the truth that it reveals, comes the conviction to take right action—the movement that keeps us on the wave.

With the practice of receiving, my intuitive vision began to awaken and come into focus. Because Spirit is the part of us that is eternal, it lives outside time and space and encompasses everything. So as my own spirit grew, so did my vision. When we see with spiritual vision, we penetrate the truth of a situation. We can see when someone is hiding something. We see their pain and we see their light, even when these things are seemingly blocked from our view. The implications of spiritual vision are tremendous. We don't use our enhanced perception to manipulate a situation in our favor, but rather to make choices that allow us to stay on our wave.

As I mentioned earlier, I've had some challenges with trusting my spiritual vision. In the beginning, I would see things but not know if I was making it up. I've heard a lot of people say this. Spiritual vision is so subtle that it's easy to dismiss. But when my hunches turned out to be accurate a TRILLION times, I started to trust myself. I had the biggest problem with men. If I was in love, I would second guess myself. Or I would ask them if what I was feeling was true. More often than not, they would side step or back step or avoid telling me all together. And more often than not, I allowed their evasiveness to confuse me and mitigate my vision. But as I said before, I've learned the hard way to trust my intuitive perceptions. I may put the wrong spin on something or attribute my perception to wrong cause, but even that has diminished as my vision gets clearer. My sisters (both biological and chosen) have helped me a lot with this and I help them. We listen to each other's hunches and validate what we can. We also encourage each other to trust ourselves. It does help to have a buddy in this process because learning to trust intuition is like learning a new language. It takes time and practice. But it is so freeing as you get better. You don't waste time with people or projects that will bog you down. I find myself "tuning in" to future events to see if they will be nourishing and fun or draining and stressful, then I decide if I will go or not. Frequently, the very perception I had is later validated by the people who've attended. I've slowly overcome this first challenge and now I try not to second guess myself.

If I'm confused or unclear about something it's usually because I'm emotionally tangled with someone else. When my intuition is muddy, I try to get calm and move into my center as soon as possible. Clarity takes time, but when we are willing and committed to see, we're shown what needs to be done in order to untangle from others and process old emotions that might be getting in the way of clear vision. This involves taking responsibility and a serious commitment to spiritual growth—not just personal growth—growth that is initiated by Spirit. This type of growth transforms us into a perfect vessel for Spirit by addressing one issue at a time. Purification can take years, even a lifetime, but it is part of the Free Spirit curriculum. Everything else is just an act.

There are a couple of caveats regarding spiritual vision. In a world of increasing transparency and connection, it is more important than ever to cultivate boundaries. This goes both ways. We need to respect other's boundaries by not always sharing what we see. It can feel like a violation to another person if we blatantly blurt out our perception. I've learned to be general. If I sense that something is wrong in another, I might say, "Is everything okay?" Or I might just give them some extra love and not say anything at all. All we can do is use our best judgment here—when intention is focused on doing everything for the highest good, we know what to do. When the ego gets involved, it wants to show off by being a know-it-all. This generates karma and doesn't bring light to the situation, so we need to be discerning and keep our ego in check. We also need to have boundaries for ourselves, being careful not to take on other's emotions, fears and moods. This is an occupational hazard of transparency. Being an open vessel, we are highly susceptible to outside energies. Again, it's so subtle that it takes time to get the feel of what energy/emotion is yours versus another's. We live in a sea of spirit and there are undercurrents of emotion everywhere. We can simply float by them and they'll latch on, particularly if we're holding a similar vibe of our own. Sometimes it's good. We get a wave of empathy and can respond compassionately, but other times it's detrimental, like catching a cold.

Emotionally speaking, if we're not careful, we can catch someone's bad mood or end up "doing" their feeling for them. Women are especially prone to this, and we have to stop—especially with our boys and men. Because we feel their emotion, we will pick it right up and process it for them in order to ease their discomfort, but this absolves the responsibility to feel their feelings and communicate. Not only does processing another's feelings bog us down or potentially drag us into a sea of darkness, it also denies the other person an opportunity to grow. It is common to enable our men by feeling their feelings for them. We know that we're taking on our man's feelings when we become over-emotional in response to him appearing under-emotional. I've done this plenty and have sworn it off.

The moment I start to feel that the wave of emotion in me is endless, I know that I'm doing someone else's work. In my case, it's usually someone close, but some people are sensitive to the point of tapping into global energies or catastrophes in other parts of the world and therefore become overwhelmed by feelings that seemingly come out of nowhere. I'm all for empathy and compassion, but beyond that I've come to believe that psychic boundaries are essential for those of us who are open and have vision.

If we can remember that emotions are contagious and it is natural to feel the energies around us, we can then protect ourselves accordingly. I've learned to just lean in, feel what's happening and then back up into my own center. That way I can be helpful and empathetic without drowning in a sea of endless emotion that isn't mine.

Rule #3: Surrender

We don't have control over Spirit any more than a surfer has control over the ocean. The ego tries to control, manipulate and mold situations into whatever makes it feel secure. The spirit surfer surrenders to the will of life. We know that like soft, white sand, we will be refined into the purest version of ourselves as we're delivered to our highest life—one that maximizes the expression of spirit through our transparent vessel. Surrendering requires us to travel lightly. Possessions, titles and the beliefs constructed to help the ego feel secure are happily traded for the freedom that comes with riding the wave of Spirit. We still have desires and preferences, but we hold them loosely and give way to emerging waves that offer greater expression of Spirit. Grace replaces rigidity when spirit surfing. We never know when the next wave will lift us up and carry us forward on a grand surge of exhilaration.

It took me a long time to learn the art of surrender, but becoming a transparent vessel meant letting go of my personal agenda. My ego fought this one tooth and nail, but eventually, as I became more attached to the peaceful feeling of a flowing spirit, I became less attached to any particular outcome that wasn't gracefully unfolding. Of course, I still have a preference with most things, but holding on too tight strangles my spirit. It can be confusing with all the messages we hear about manifesting our dreams, but truly, my experience has been that the tighter I hold on, the less likely I am to achieve my desires. When I started my writing career, I was sure that I would be a bestselling author. There wasn't a doubt in my mind. I believed it would happen very fast. But my career didn't immediately take off, instead it expanded gradually, the way a planted seed grows and blossoms in its own time. One night early in my career I had a dream. I was on a bike ride with Oprah and Barbara Streisand. We were having a great time riding our cruisers and chatting about life, but then people started interrupting our ride and wanting to talk. We had to stop our bikes and talk to them and then start again. It was frustrating and taking away from the carefree joy of the bike ride. Then I heard a voice. It was so loud that it woke me up. It said, "BE CAREFUL WHAT YOU WISH FOR." This dream changed the way

I thought about success. It helped me understand that I needed more time to develop myself and my ability to be a free spirit under all circumstances. Had my first book blown up the way I expected it to, my growth would have been interrupted and I may not have ever gotten to this point of freedom and inner peace. I'm now grateful that everything has unfolded gradually so that I had time to fully develop. Spirit knows what our minds and egos don't. And when we surrender to its will above all else, the path that leads to maximal spiritual expression lights up before us. Of course, we have free will and can choose to manipulate events to our ego's liking, but if we hold on to the need to control the events in our lives, we won't be free spirits. At a point we have to choose to either ride the wave of Spirit or paddle our little butts like crazy to get to a destination that we think will make us happy.

Rule # 4: Be Fearless

Like a giant wave, Spirit destroys everything that resists its momentum. Fear of processing old emotion or trying something new can cause us to avoid and resist the waves of Spirit that seek to move through us. Resistance causes pain, however, and will only make our journey more difficult. Allow yourself to be cleared of any internal debris and move in the direction that you're guided so that spirit can flow through you like a tidal wave.

Over time, the waves of life wash away our fear of drowning. We realize that we aren't just surfing on the water, but that we are the water and drowning is impossible. We don't know this until we surrender, however, because prior to surrendering, we remain terrified of annihilation, and rightly so. I recently stumbled upon a quote by Adyashanti that started with this, "Make no mistake about it, enlightenment is a destructive process..." I couldn't agree more. Spirit destroys everything blocking its expression, which can make us feel desperate and afraid. This is normal, as parts of us do die when we surrender, but only the parts that we have constructed to protect us against the transformative nature of Spirit.

We always have the choice to listen to our intuition and take the small (or big) steps that support our growth. Adopting fearlessness and taking these steps "recommended" by our intuition makes transformation way easier. The life of a free spirit is characterized by short bouts of tension (transformation) followed by long bouts of peace (free flowing spirit). If we refuse to do what we know in our heart is best, transformation still occurs, but it feels more like getting thrown off your surf board every 30 seconds than catching a wave and riding it to shore. Some poor souls even make the ultimate mistake of trying to control life by delaying their own transformation until death. But the price for this level of ego control is too big to articulate and makes for a life riddled with fear where inner freedom and peace remain elusive. Very sad existence indeed. God bless the people who are too afraid to surrender. Spirit surfing involves listening within and receiving very explicit instructions on how to collaborate with Spirit.

The saying "feel the fear and do it anyway" applies here because whether we choose to collaborate or not, we will experience fear, with the only difference being that fear goes away once we catch that wave by doing what we need to do despite the natural hesitation we all experience. I can't tell you how many times my intuition has told me to do a certain thing – stand up and speak my truth or make a simple diet change—to which I responded by digging my heals into the ground day after day in a resistant pout. At some level you just know when you're about to enter the fire of transformation and that even the smallest modifications in behavior can feel frightening. It is as if Spirit says, "Stop. Move over. Let me in. It won't hurt. You just think it will." But from a human perspective, it does hurt for a minute when a piece of you is burned off to make more room for Spirit. We feel the tension, the craving, the desire to do whatever it is we have done in the past. But it gets easier when we know what to expect. The Modern Hippie has learned how to walk into the fire of transformation when necessary.

Rule #5: Don't Wait

Help everyone you can along the way. It will only make your wave bigger. But don't try and wait for those who are not ready. You will suffer and Spirit will have one less vessel to flow through. There will be those who are still learning to surf. Know that we are all connected and your beautiful surfing will help inspire them to do the same. There will be times on your own journey when you feel lost. Rest if you must but never give up. If you don't know what you're doing or where you're going, it means that you need to receive more – in the receiving you will be shown how to get back on the wave.

"Don't Wait" is one of my favorite rules of spirit surfing. I think it resonates so much because of how much time I've spent waiting for others. It's easy to get confused when the rules of society mingle with the rules of Spirit. Society tells us to commit and to keep our word. It urges us not to give up on people, and all this is good, to a point... The mass ascension that humanity is experiencing right now—the rapid clearing and preparing of our containers to channel ever increasing amounts of spiritual energy—does not support waiting for others to get on board. Again, we can wait if we choose, but there's a price to be paid for that choice. The price is depression (the pressing down of spirit) or anxiety (one's spirit frantically swimming in circles). Or, while waiting, we can easily fall into an addiction (chasing spirit) as we innocently try to numb ourselves to the pain of avoiding our own spirit.

I've had to come to terms with the fact that the ten or more years that I chose to linger in relationships that weren't going anywhere had a purpose. Perhaps I needed that time to become stronger and learn how to trust myself. My experience is that the energy that I lost while waiting for my partner to spirit surf with me returned one painful piece at a time once the relationship ended, ultimately propelling me to my rightful place vibrationally. But standing still takes its toll, as it's draining and confusing. As I was "waiting" for my relationship to evolve with Man #3, I had a dream that the two of us were living inside a Volkswagen bus. Everyone else was living outside. Another man whom I love and respect came and knocked on the window of the bus. I opened the window and poked my head out. I was so happy to see him. He told me that the window of opportunity was closing and that I needed to come out of the bus and live the life I was supposed to be living. It would be another three years before I got out of that bus.

While waiting too long for someone temporarily costs us our freedom, helping others who are ready for help lifts up all of us. Spirit surfers offer help without even thinking. We are either guided or inspired or it just happens. There are so many living beings (people, animals, bugs, plants) that cross our paths. Sometimes we lend them a hand and sometimes they lend us a hand. I'm certainly grateful for all who have helped me up when I was down or helped me go higher when I was up! Helping others nourishes the spirit like nothing else as long as the person is ready for our help. If not, we should send them a big dose of love and keep moving.

Rule #6: Steer Clear

Steer clear of those who would bring you down. They will be holding out candy and cold beer, but your heart will tell you if they are floating egos who consume others for lunch. Keep going. Don't be lured by shiny objects.

When we get to this point of transparency and vision, we are able to discern those who present emotional or physical danger. As a young girl, I would gravitate toward emotionally dangerous people thinking I could rescue them. That's child play. God rescues, not us, and even then, the person needs to be willing. These days my instincts take over and I naturally surf around danger. Sometimes I surf by the danger or negativity so fast that it doesn't even register in my awareness. When it does, I say a prayer.

Rule #7: Celebrate

Celebrate those who are in front of you and above you. You might be riding a small wave compared to someone else, but there are many unseen factors that affect one's journey. Something might be brewing underneath you that you have yet to perceive. By focusing on what you don't have, you diminish the good that's on its way. Focus solely on the wave that you're on and give a nod of approval to all who pass you.

At first the ego resists celebrating others who are ahead of us or above us. It's the old programming that tells us that the pie is only so big and if someone else has a big piece of your favorite pie then there's only a little left for you. We know better now, that love begets love, abundance begets abundance and success begets success. When envy sneaks into my awareness, I try to quickly transform it into admiration and ask myself how I can cultivate that same quality within myself. Most of the time I'm able to appreciate the infinite variations of beauty and abundance that surround us, but sometimes I need to be reminded there's always enough to go around. Once when I was feeling particularly unappreciated, I asked Spirit for some perspective. I was given "a talking to" of sorts. Spirit said, "Do you see the beauty in the grass you're walking on? What about the trees that surround you? What about the beauty in the eyes of everyone you look upon? My dear, under-appreciation is a human epidemic." Point taken... It's easy to forget to appreciate the thousands of faces of God that we encounter every day, but remembering to do so feels so good.

Enjoy the Ride

With these seven rules of spirit surfing, I'm reminded that life is about the journey, not the destination. It's not about getting to the shore; it's about bringing balance and presence into each moment. It's not about finding that perfect job, spouse... fill in the blank, it's about being where you're at in every moment, using vision and grace to navigate. Shifting from outcome orientation to process orientation is one of the most difficult things to do, but I find when I relax into the present, something very heavy falls off my shoulders and is replaced by calm, expansive energy in my belly. I've noticed that the most enlightened among us are able to see perfection in the midst of imperfection. The saying, "It's all good" takes on a whole new meaning. It really is all good. We can either accept this moment and remain open or resist, run from or defend against the present, shutting out our spirit. Spirit surfing involves remaining open regardless of our present circumstances and feelings. I'm noticing that processing difficult emotions that arise is infinitely easier than blocking them. I would much rather feel the quick sting of a difficult or unpleasant feeling than remain cut off from my essence my entire life. Once we're on the road to transparency, the heaviness of sup-pressed emotion becomes an unbearable weight. Spirit surfing requires us to be where we're at even when the waves are choppy and overwhelming. By remaining present, alert and engaged, we move through the rough spots quicker so that we can once again enjoy the ride.

The rules of spirit surfing promise to elevate us to a life that is grander than anything we could create on our own. As we receive our own spirit and surrender to it, we are shown how to fearlessly navigate our journey. We help who we can and pray for those we can't and move past anyone who would otherwise bring us down. We celebrate all who accompany us on our journey and commit to the process of becoming a transparent vessel for spirit. As a result, we are free.

Chapter 7

Freedom in Rituals

The other day as I was walking Mucci, my black, dread lock-sporting cockapoo, I ran into a woman named Linda and her dog Cody. This is the first time I've become a part of a dog community where everyone knows the dog's names but not the people's... If you're a dog person, you know what I'm talking about. So although we'd met before, I couldn't remember her name. After reintroducing ourselves, we start walking together while our dogs alternate between sniffing around and running in the lush green grass. When I mention that I'm writing a book about hippies, she lights up like a Christmas tree. "Oh wow, I grew up in the '60s on the East Coast. We were a part of the Woodstock generation... listening to music, dropping acid and protesting the Vietnam War."

Then I light up like a Christmas tree, "Really? So what was it like? Who were your favorite bands? Do you still smoke pot?" She does by the way. At sixty-five, she's as fresh as the daisy she wore in her hair and is not afraid to pull out her pipe. We ended up getting together a few days later for a glass of wine and a swim in her pool—with Cody and Mucci, of course. I arrive to find her in a bathing suit sweeping her back patio. She has legs that come up to my waist and straight, longish hair. It's not a stretch to picture her in the 1960s, but when she gives me a tour of her house, I spot an old picture of her and her brother, which completely solidified my vision. Her hair is a lot longer and she's gazing at the camera wearing John Lennon glasses. It's brilliant. Aside from simply enjoying her company, which I did immensely, I wanted to talk more about the rituals that hippies used to free their spirits.

I start our conversation asking about her favorite bands. She mentions The Grateful Dead, Frank Zappa and Jefferson Airplane. And of course, she loved the Beatles. "Everyone did," She said. "In a way, they led the whole movement." She went on to explain that young America followed their lead the way a field of grain sways in the wind. Then we moved on to drugs. Oh, yeah... we dropped acid every Friday night." I ask if it expanded her consciousness. "YES! To this day!" I silently get a little acid envy and wonder why I've done it the hard way all these years...

"And we smoked pot regularly." She proceeds to tell me that she took a few tokes before I arrived to get in the right frame of mind for our conversation. I ask about yoga and meditation and she says, "Yep, thanks to The Beatles." Their brief stint with Maharishi Mahesh Yogi, the man who introduced Transcendental Meditation to the West, ignited a meditation movement that's stronger than ever today. She puts yoga in the same category as meditation – part of the same wave that brought Eastern traditions over to the West. Linda shares memories of protesting the war with her long-haired boyfriend who had been in Special Forces in Vietnam and returned with his eyes wide open to the futility of it all.

"Speaking of your boyfriend..." I ask, "What about free love?"

"My friends and I mostly stuck with our own partners, but there were people who were very free with their love. Everyone was different and that's fine! Freedom is what we were about—everyone did whatever they wanted and no one judged." I leave Linda's house, not only with a new kindred spirit, but an even deeper appreciation for the '60s and how much these hippies directly influenced my own life. It used to be that these yoga practicing, concert goers were considered seriously "out there" by their more conservative counterparts, but thankfully this is no longer true. Meditation, yoga and music festivals are now mainstream and have become the way I practice my religion. They are the rituals that invoke my spirit and sense of freedom. I'm a big believer in rituals. They've been around since the beginning of time and provide a sacred form through which spirit can flow.

Both meditation and yoga are non-negotiable parts of my life. Meditation is my life-line and yoga is my anti-depressant. I don't know what I would do without the spiritual support that I receive every morning in meditation. It nourishes me, guides me and carries me. I also have this strong sense that it buffers and protects me. Each morning I sit in silence as spirit fills my body; it then navigates my travels throughout the day and keeps me out of harm's way. I am not a perfect meditator (or perfect anything for that matter), as thoughts constantly creep in and I have to move myself back into silence what seems like a hundred times during my twenty to thirty minute session. But Spirit doesn't require perfection, just willingness and a little effort. As I've shared, I'm grateful and couldn't live without this life-giving ritual.

While meditation is like drinking life, yoga is like bathing in a holy river. It removes all the mental, emotional and physical impurities that I've collected throughout the day. I don't joke when I say it's my anti-depressant either, as I always step off my mat feeling lighter and more free than when I stepped on it. I got hooked on hot yoga shortly after my spiritual awakening for the detox feeling that it provides, and although I really enjoy other forms of hatha yoga, I seem to always return to the heat. I know it's not for everyone, especially people who have an aversion to heat, but it balances out my kapha (earth & water) body type. While I typically attend two or three classes a week, I once did thirty classes in thirty days. I was in the midst of a transition and remember lying in Savasana at the end of class one day thinking, *I need to do a lot of this right now.* It is not my personality to get extreme with anything, but sometimes intuition asks us to do things outside of our comfort zone. Believe me when I tell you that at the end of thirty days I was a different person. Instead of shedding stress and negativity from the day, it felt like I let go of ten years of emotional/physical residue. God bless sweat.

Perhaps the Modern Hippie carries a yoga mat and wears her hair in a high bun, as I have yet to find a better way to prepare the body and mind to channel a spirit that's free.

The Rhythm of Life

If there's one thread that seems to weave my life together, it's music. I remember being at a Commodores concert in the early '80s where they sang a song called, "Jesus is Love." Imagine Lionel Richie's voice serenading thousands of open hearts about love. We were all singing along with the band and receiving the sermon that night. My dad was an intellectual and my mom grew up in the Science of Mind church, so there wasn't a lot of Jesus talk around my house. But when I heard that song, it resonated as truth. Perhaps it was the spirit of love in the arena that night that compelled me to rush home and plead with my mom to get me that album as soon as possible—yes, album—which we did, the very next day. Music is vibration, and as I will share in the next chapter, it has awakened

my spirit and healed my heart. Music is a powerful and worldwide ritual. Whether drumming,
chanting, a long Grateful Dead jam or the sweet
voice of Lionel Richie, music moves the spirit to
the point that it becomes physically impossible to
remain still.

Modern Love

Let's face it: love is still pretty free in our cul-
ture. Just like Linda's experience in the '60s, most
of us tend to "stick with our own partners." However, changing partners is as easy as getting a
fresh piece of gum when your last piece has lost its
flavor. So what does a relationship look like for the
free spirit? Is marriage still relevant? What are the
rules for conscious relating? What's coming to me
is that the only rule is to be true to oneself. Like to
swing? The more the merrier. Prefer a more traditional lifestyle in a deeply committed relationship?
Get married! As a healer/philosopher type, it's
been important for me to sort this out personally
as well as collectively. On a personal level, even
though I value monogamy and would never want
to be in an open relationship, I'm only interested in
relationships that *feel* free and elevated—the way
I feel when I'm single. This has been challenging

at times because of my deep fear of loss when I'm in love (aka, abandonment issues). Fear and courage don't mix well, and feeling free requires that we courageously follow our hearts, even when our actions bring up fear or disappoint a lover. Thankfully, my courage has grown in direct proportion to my spirit and preserving my integrity is now more important to me than holding on to any particular form—even if he looks like George Clooney. Being true to one's spirit doesn't always involve walking away from a lover, however. I had lunch with a dear friend yesterday who was able to reclaim her spirit just by standing up for herself when her husband got angry over burnt bacon. It may not seem like a spirit-recapturing moment, but believe me, there are plenty of men and women who forsake their spirit just to keep the peace. Here's the thing about being a free spirit: we don't know where the wave is going to take us. We can't be both a free spirit and be tethered to particular form. We just have to trust that if we do what our hearts tell us to do at every turn, we will end up at the right destination.

Despite my life-long ride on the roller coaster of love, I see this as a promising time for relationships. Modern love is first and foremost, transparent. Granted, this is true only for those of us who've allowed Spirit to buff us into transparency. There are still many people living in a dense vibration where they are not yet able to perceive their own spiritual guidance much less able to penetrate the truth of those around them. This is unfortunate, but the wave of Spirit never stops and they will eventually be on it. For those of us living in the age of transparency or on our way, we are not only able to see others in a deeper way but we are committed to allowing others to see us. Not being transparent hurts. Just think about the last time you carried a shameful secret. It feels like carrying a bowling ball full of poison in the belly, doesn't it?

As Modern Hippies, we are honest. We seem compelled—we are compelled—to preserve our transparency by sharing our truth. It's emotional honesty more than anything. Being clear and untangled, the spirit within us can feel when a lover is holding on to something and our lover can feel when we are holding on to something. Perhaps we say just a little, if we ourselves are in the midst of some emotional confusion, but we do say something because we care about the soul who's in front of us. We lovingly share our truth even when it's hard to say. This is where courage comes in. Little boys and girls who are still afraid of getting in trouble with their mommies have no business being in relationships—at least not with Modern Hippies.

But what about how quickly things change when you're riding the spirit wave? Modern love is dynamic if nothing else. It ebbs and flows in the short term and changes seasons in the long term. Let's say that you marry Handsome Joe from high school, and twenty-five years later you find your essence wanting to flow into a different vibe? These types of situations can be so confusing. They bring us face to face with the conflict between being a free spirit and honoring family and societal traditions. But truly, our only task is to maintain transparency by keeping our eyes wide open (even though denial can be *so* comforting) and honoring ourselves by speaking our truth. Spirit takes care of the rest. If the relationship needs to unravel, it unravels. If it needs to transform or grow, it does. But only when we do our part by keeping our eyes open and compassionately sharing our truth. When we relate the old way—avoiding conflict, acting how we think we "should," etc., we stunt our growth and lose spiritual freedom and inner peace.

I've found that the journey to transparency resembles healthy eating. Once you start, it feels really crumby to backslide and that donut doesn't even taste good any more. At a point, it becomes impossible to ignore one's spirit and that, in my humble opinion, is a good thing. Perhaps we're moving closer to unconditional love? Until I reclaimed my spirit and sorted through my huge pile of inner rubbish, I wasn't able to really love a man. Instead, my love was simply projected (the opposite of expressed) onto these unsuspecting souls, leaving them with the impossible task of giving it back to me. Herein lies the difference between conditional and unconditional love. Conditional love is merely the swapping of projections... "You be my knight in shining armor and I'll be you're perfect princess." When either party fails to live up to the agreement, disillusionment sets in—the illusion is dismantled. But the Modern Hippie is herself a river of love! Yes, she enjoys merging with another river, but when the other river veers off for a moment, or even forever, panic doesn't set in because the love flowing through her is endless. Unconditional love doesn't ask us to give up limits or boundaries on behavior, just to remember that attempting to manipulate others in order to feel loved or secure only imprisons ourselves. There's no reason to try to control one another—the love we receive is the love we give and it is there all the time.

Chapter 8

Resonance

On one of the last cool evenings of spring, my friend Julie and I decide to meet up at the local coffee shop. We take a seat on the patio overlooking the greenbelt, which is a grassy wash that runs through the city in order to catch excess rain water and prevent flooding. But along with having a practical function, the greenbelt provides a refreshing oasis in the midst of our natural desert landscape. There's a slight breeze and our characteristic bright blue sky is changing to a deep indigo as the sun sets. You have to seize spring weather in Phoenix because once it turns hot, there's no going back for a solid three to four months. My friend and I are passionately discussing spirituality and how the world is changing until we both get distracted by a handsome man walking by with his massive black dog. Only he doesn't end up walking by because we all catch each other's vibe and he casually walks toward us. The three of us strike up a conversation and it turns out he's just returned from a year and a half of traveling, simultaneously exploring his outer and inner worlds. He shares that in his experience, people are awakening all over the planet – exactly what my friend and I were just saying. After talking for about thirty minutes, we reflect on the serendipity of our seemingly random encounter. "It's vibration soup" I say, as we all nod in amazement... Indeed, vibration soup.

There are no accidents. We flow into the areas that resonate with our being and stay until we're inspired to gracefully flow into another vibe. With spirit at the surface of our awareness, we're led to the exact person, place or situation that has the potential to either elevate or heal us. The three of us coming together to talk about how the world is healing was just one of a thousand elevating and validating experiences.

Our spirit also directs us toward those individuals or situations that activate old emotion or trauma that's ready to be healed and released. And we are serendipitously drawn to those who awaken unrealized aspects of our personality, inspiring us to cultivate our gifts. All of these vibrational opportunities are designed to move us toward wholeness, thereby preparing us for increased spiritual expression and freedom. I find the fact that we live in a vibrational world exciting, and knowing that the outer world reflects my inner world helps me take responsibility for my own evolution. Yet there are so many of us that stay perpetually distracted from our own spirit by being tied to electronics or on a constant treadmill of work or personal drama. To ignore outer signs and neglect our inner voice is to remain a robot instead of becoming a Modern Hippie. For some, having this level of heightened awareness feels like a burden or extra responsibility, for it is impossible to remain in denial and avoid Right Action when we tune into all that Spirit reveals. But it's a lot like trekking up a steep, snowy mountain in order to ski down. It's so worth it!

Wander in Wonder

When we begin to accept all of the aspects of ourselves that the universe reflects, we increase our flow and the ability to effortlessly move into vibrational situations that bring magic and wonder into our lives. When was the last time you wandered around wide-eyed and open-hearted in a state of wonder? This might very well be my favorite state of mind, as I've found it to be the perfect formula for getting in the divine flow of vibrational soup. Magical things, like my friend and I meeting the man with the dog, happen while in this state. That evening, he was wandering with wonder and stumbled upon us! I see wandering as being pliable enough to change your direction in any given moment and having a sense of wonder as being like a child—open, innocent, non-judgmental and viewing the world as if you're looking at it for the first time. Spirit can most easily lead us toward serendipitous events and like-minded people when we're in this state.

I once went to a Ziggy Marley concert. I had gotten my ticket in the general admission area so that I could sit with my friends, but in my heart I really wanted to be closer and thought about it many times before the show. The day of the concert, I had to work late and ended up driving on my own. I arrived to find hundreds of people in line waiting to pick up tickets at will call. Oblivious to the fact that it was going to take at least 45 minutes to get my ticket and the show would have already started by the time I reached my friends, I stood in line with a calm mind, an open heart and a positive spirit. People around me were smoking and complaining but for some reason my vibration just wouldn't dip. I was in line for no more than five minutes when a guy walked straight up to me and said, "Hey, do you need a ticket?"

"What kind of ticket?" I ask, with hopeful optimism.

"It's a VIP pass for the front; I'm leaving."

"Well, yes! Actually! How much do you want for it?"

"Nothing, it was given to me and I'm leaving."

"Can I just give you $20.00 bucks?" I ask, knowing full well that it's a 75.00 dollar ticket.

"No really, it's fine. Have fun!" He takes the VIP pass off from around his neck, hands it to me and walks away. I proceed to prance off to find my friends only to give them hugs before heading to the front row where I enjoyed the entire concert! This actually happened again several months later when I was out of town, only this time the concert I wanted to go to was sold out and a stranger randomly offered me a ticket in the elevator of a nearby hotel. He said his friend couldn't make it and, once again, wouldn't accept a dollar for it.

Wandering in a state of wonder captures the free spirit mentality more than anything; it's the ability to detach enough from your own agenda and allow Spirit to carry you, without any effort, to the perfect destination. Can you imagine living an entire life like this? Sounds a lot like the effortless application of the law of attraction—having natural desires, releasing them, and then being completely present to whatever unfolds. When we hold on to our desires with tight fists, our whole body contracts and Spirit can't work its magic.

Remembering

Vibrational resonance often brings us face to face with souls we've loved in past lives. We can't put our finger on it, but every now and then a stranger feels familiar. We are often compelled to move toward them and complete whatever we started the last time we were together. Past lovers may or may not reunite, but the opportunity to complete the karmic journey is always present. My journey toward freedom required me to transmute the crippling pattern of longing for a lover who wasn't there, and the perfect opportunity to do so presented itself in the form of a traveling musician.

I heard one of his songs on a mixed CD that my sister-in-law gave me. The song resonated with my soul and I decided to check out the band's upcoming performance with her and my brother. Having no idea what to expect, we arrive at a smaller venue with no seats so that everyone can stand around and dance. We get a drink and talk for a few minutes while waiting for the show to start. Soon the music starts playing and the lead singer walks on to the stage. The strangest thing happens... His presence confuses me. He's familiar and foreign all at the same time. I'm suspended in what feels like a mild state of shock for a few moments before finally adjusting. Have you ever experienced that, when someone's presence takes you off guard to the point of freezing your perception so that you're unable to process what's in front of you? I eventually relax and enjoy the show, despite the surreal beginning.

I get separated from my brother and sister-in-law toward the end of the evening and find myself wandering around looking for them when the show was over. As I make my way to the lobby, I notice the lead singer surrounded by a group of people. I see him glance at me from across the lobby and I decide to slowly walk over. As I approach, he comes out from the middle of the crowd and greets me with, "Hello my sister" and leans in for a hug...vibrational soup. We exchange a little small talk and then I spot my sister-in-law and walk over to her.

"Oh my God, he recognized you!" she exclaims. I'm not sure what she meant by that or if she even knows. All I know is that he had me at *hello my sister.* This guy got stuck in my psyche. About a year after that first show, I went on a vacation to the beach. The ocean tends to open channels of intuition like only nature can; it's as if the power of the vast sea dissolves the barrier between the unconscious and conscious mind. On this particular afternoon, I'm sitting on the sand looking at the sparkly blue water thinking about nothing in particular when it hits me. *He's the man from my past life who was sent away.* This insight carried a level of conviction that I'd come to recognize as intuition. This isn't something that I wanted to be true or that I'd even considered. In fact, the entire notion was so far out there that I was hesitant to even tell anyone, but would eventually tell my sisters and best friends.

Before I decided to rely solely on my own intuition for guidance, I would occasionally treat myself to a reading from a highly intuitive woman who channels the angels. She's a beautiful soul who shares things like my daughter is a leader on the playground and is going to travel the world when she gets older. Most of the time, I enjoyed the visits more for the loving validation than anything else. But on this particular visit I decide to ask about the traveling musician. I didn't tell her anything about him except for his first name. She tunes in and says, "Wow, you guys had a passionate love affair in a past life. *Really passionate!*" Then she goes on to say something that I will never forget.

"It looks like you freed each other. You freed him to be himself in a much bigger way and he freed you from lifetimes of conforming." This matched my past life regression exactly. He was freed from the insane bondage of slavery never to be seen again, and I broke out of the traditional, stiff, upper-class mold that I'd been living for God knows how long.

Past life encounters are mysterious and often lead to more questions than answers, but what I do know is that his presence activated centuries-old buried emotion that needed to be healed in order for me to quit making choices based on fear of abandonment. For several years following that initial encounter, longing swirled within me like a tornado that kept gaining momentum. And because he was out of reach, my only choice was to look at the truth of my pain, feel it, and release it while continuing to strengthen the connection to my own spirit—our only source of real security.

My dad once told me that he views me as a rebellious soul who always pushed the social envelope growing up, "kind of like the bikers of the '60s." Being somewhat of a renegade himself, he shared his observations from a place of love and respect. What he's saying is true. I've lived an unconventional life and I wouldn't have it any other way. If it weren't for breaking out of that conforming mold in my last life, perhaps I would be locked into society's rules again in this life. The truth is, my lover in that life wasn't the only slave, we were both slaves and we did free each other. Having my past life activated by the presence of this musician helped me to finally release the pattern of longing for love even when it's right in front of me. My healing also helped me transform the fear of loss that led me to cling to men who weren't right for me the way a fearful child clings to her mother when she could be out playing with her friends.

I share this because it's been a big part of my journey toward becoming a free spirit. Until I remembered my past life, a piece of my spirit was lost—it left that summer day on the plantation hundreds of years ago. *A fragmented spirit leaves one wanting*. When a spirit is shattered in trauma, it's often propelled in different directions. Sometimes a piece is lost to a lover or abusing family member—we literally lose a piece of ourselves. Other times it gets buried deep within our psyches underneath a pile of pain. But even though a piece of me was lost, it was still mine and the infinite organizing power of Spirit always leads us directly to the people, places and situations that provide the perfect opportunity for integration. I was brought face to face with the man who was able to help me reclaim the missing fragment of my spirit.

It's easy to think that the only way to get our spirit back is through a redo—going back and doing it all over again. This is why we repeat patterns with lovers over and over; we're attempting to reclaim what we've lost and believe that only they can give us back our power. The reality is that lost pieces of our spirit can only be reclaimed from within. But we often avoid this direct route to wholeness because integrating a piece of ourselves involves feeling the pain that caused our spirit to fragment in the first place. It is by courageously going into that deep dark cave that we've avoided for so long that we find the very thing we thought that only the world could provide. Once we get the courage to journey out of our comfort zone and into the unknown—often portrayed so beautifully in children's movies with the protagonist leaving the safety of home only to end up in the wilderness alone and afraid—we emerge from our inner adventure renewed and whole. We fortify our strengthened spirit by making empowering choices rather than repeating the pattern that caused us to lose a piece of ourselves in the first place.

Sometime after the activation and integration of my fragmented spirit, I found myself feeling insecure again, the way we feel when we're not whole. I intuitively ask, "Is there any piece of me still missing?" I'm guided to do a scan where I tune in to all the people I've loved to see where I still feel a strong charge. As I scan each of my lovers in this life and the last, I feel neutrality with each until I reach the traveling musician. The charge is palpable. It feels like heat and tingling in my belly. *Ah, of course, a piece of me is still with him.* I then go into meditation and declare that I'm ready to retrieve my spirit. I sense that my past lover will feel a little lighter, so I'm able to proceed, knowing it will be beneficial for both of us. I ask Archangel Michael to help me. Within seconds, I feel my body jerk in a quick, reflexive manner and my abdomen sucks in as if catching something. I then become completely still. After a moment or two of settling, I silently welcome my spirit home.

In the weeks following this experience I would become aware of several other pieces of my spirit needing retrieval. It turns out that, as with all healing, my attention initially went to the area that had the most charge. Once I had the palpable experience of having a piece of my spirit returned, clues emerged as to where to find the final fragments. One clue was a dream I had where I was waiting for an ex-lover to pick me up and he never showed. When I woke up it dawned on me that a piece of me was still with him. So as I went in to meditation that morning, I repeated the same process of becoming very still and receptive, declaring that I was ready to retrieve that piece of my spirit and then asking Archangel Michael for help. The same exact thing occurred with the physical jerk in my belly. I invoked this integrating ritual two more times after receiving clues and intuitive hunches on the whereabouts of my scattered spirit. What I notice now is sense of peaceful wholeness that I have never felt in this lifetime. Truly, as *A Course in Miracles* states, "I am in need of nothing but the truth." My chase is finally over.

The last time I saw the traveling musician at one of his shows, I was anticipating the familiar surge of electricity and emotion that always coursed through my body upon seeing him. But this time was different, when he walked onto the stage, the electricity and emotion was replaced by calm, fun energy—the kind of emotion you expect to experience at a concert by a musician you enjoy. At the end of the show he mingled with the crowd as he always does. The scene was crazy and chaotic, so I decided to reach in for a fist bump and call it a night. I extended my arm through the crowd and gave him a nod and a smile. He reached back and bumped my fist. There was no recognition or emotional charge, just a friendly exchange with a fan. The karma had been transmuted into complete neutrality. While a part of me felt sad that this dramatic spiritual dance was over, I mostly felt freed and ready to move on to a new chapter of my life. Sometimes we get to reincarnate without ever dying. We get to start fresh with a clean slate entirely free from karmic ties. As I've mentioned, I like the idea of zero karma. I see zero karma as transcending both bad and good patterns. It is a place of freedom where all the ribbons of energy have been untangled from one's past and present relationships. I'm pretty sure I have some karma left to untangle in other areas of my life, and I'm working on that, but relationally, I feel very free.

The most direct path to freedom is revealed by

our spirit, but only if we choose to listen. This process sometimes activates intense desire, and other times, intense sadness. We don't just get up one day, part our hair down the middle and declare ourselves to be a Modern Hippie. This level of carefree joy and liberation is earned through a devotion to Spirit that's greater than any other urge within oneself. Eventually, when we are clear and wholly integrated, Spirit is able to flow in any direction that it desires like a powerful, raging river. We are free.

Reconnecting

Two decades after my spiritual awakening I receive notice of my thirty-year high school reunion. I've known many of these people since I was five years old and just the thought of seeing them gives me the jitters. We started kindergarten together. They witnessed me sitting on the sidelines painfully wishing I was more like my outgoing friends.

I decide to wear a beautiful red lace dress with jagged edges like a fairy. It's more artsy than sexy, and I love it. I put my hair in a top not, put on a pastel, pink lipstick reminiscent of the '60s, and wear the gold hoop earrings I bought from my extraordinarily talented friend Karen who will be there. The reunion begins on the rooftop of a local hotel where you can see the mountains surrounding the valley—Camelback to the right and Papago to the left. I arrive a little late and the sun is quickly setting, but hues of purple and orange still softly line the horizon. My besties are there along with a lot of the "kids" we went to school with. Everyone's all grown up—impressively so. We've done well for ourselves it seems. We sip our drinks and soak in the energy of dusk, while snapping pictures, hoping to get that perfect group shot with the sunset backdrop. After about an hour, we move downstairs for appetizers, more drinks, and yes, dancing. I talk to my best friends, I mean security blankets, beforehand. "Okay you guys, if The Hustle comes on we all have to get on the dance floor together like we did in high school okay?!" They reassure me the way they always do that they will be there for me like they've always been.

I discover the mashed potato bar and have to pinch myself, *a mashed potato bar, really? Have I died and gone to heaven?* The DJ is playing music from the '70s and '80s—Journey, AC/DC, and of course, Michael Jackson. No one is dancing though. We're all too busy chatting and enthusiastically recapturing the energy of our youth.

Then it happens. I hear the intro to The Hustle. *Do doo doo doo doo doo doo doo...* I look around and see none of my friends that I made the pact with—somehow, they've all migrated to the patio. A surge of anxiety races through my body... *What do I do? I may never get this opportunity again!* I take a deep breath and decide to go it alone. I hesitantly step onto the dance floor while looking around, still seeing no one. With no one to nestle in between, I take a deep breath and start. Right foot up twice, back twice... step to the right, step to the left... twirl... Feeling supremely self-conscious, I look up and see the two DJ's quickly glance down as if it's too painful to even watch. Just then I see one of my besties, Bridget, running toward me.

"I heard the song Kimmy! I'm coming!"

With childlike excitement, we begin to step in unison. One after another, our friends jump on to the dance floor. Before you know it, there are fifteen 48-year old women doing the hustle. Just like thirty years before, the boys line the dance floor to watch, only this time they're snapping pictures. As we dance, my spirit soars. *So this is what it feels like to be free.* I seem to grow *way* bigger than my body, my spirit surrounding the dance floor and then extending to our loving friends who are watching. Suddenly, the self-conscious little girl is gone and replaced by a grown woman with expanded consciousness. As a sea of beings moving together, our spirits join, celebrating life, our friendships, and our past. Everything is the same and yet everything is different: I no longer need my security blankets. I'm strong enough to stand, even dance, on my own two feet. The rest of the night is spent on the dance floor—hearts wide open—having some good, old-fashioned fun.

I realized that night that Spirit has a rhythm just like everything else. The ocean ebbs and flows, the sun rises and sets, we inhale and exhale, and our spirit contracts and expands. There were many times as a child that my spirit expanded beyond my body. It expanded on my walks to school as I spoke to the cacti and shrubs that lined the sidewalk. It expanded as my friends and I laughed hysterically in our bedrooms during sleepovers. And it expanded and contracted over and over with lovers who would eventually usher me back to myself. I realized that Spirit always has our back, and for those of us like me that spent a little too much time contracted, it eventually expands us enough so that the ebb and flow becomes rhythmic and organic. My task in this lifetime has been to allow Spirit to break down the massive walls that were carefully constructed to protect my fragile, innocent heart. Now, with an open heart and a spirit that's free, the Modern Hippie in me knows that trying to stay expanded all the time would be like trying to inhale all the time. Just like the exhale makes space for the fresh inhale, spiritual contraction builds intensity that gently, and sometimes forcefully, moves us toward greater expansion and freedom.

Acknowledgments

This book took nearly eight years to write. Every time I would start, something held me back. But this time around, the words poured out of me. The story was ready to be told. Like many writers, once the first draft is finished, I exhale and believe that my work is substantially done. In reality, it's only just beginning. Bringing the first draft of this book to the last involved a group of people who shared their hearts, souls, time and energy with me. All gifts that I will never forget.

Hal Zina Bennett, author of *Write from the Heart* and many other books, was the first person to look at this manuscript. He had reviewed my first book, *Opening to Life*, and always provides invaluable feedback. I simply wanted to know, "Does this story resonate?" He gave me a supportive thumbs up and some nuggets to tighten up the writing. Thank you Hal. I appreciate you, your wisdom and all that you do for the writing community.

Then enters Susan Moore, an English Professor and dear friend, "Let me take a look at your manuscript, it's what I do!" Well, she took a look at it alright—every single page. She asked me hard questions, "Is this what you mean?" "Is this the tone you really want to share with your readers?" Susan, you made this a better book on so many levels, and I'm so grateful.

My two sisters, Michelle and Kristine cannot go without mention here. We walk through this life together, arm in arm, supporting each other in everything that we do. Michelle, thank you for always seeing in me what I'm unable to see in myself. We were destined to do something sacred and meaningful together. We got this!

Kristine, I don't know where to start. You were committed to get this book right, and we did. You diligently combed through each page, untangling every sentence until the story flowed. Thank you my brilliant sister and loving friend for everything you are and everything you do.

Every now and then an angel comes along and makes your life infinitely better. Bryn Starr Best, you are that angel. Your meticulous formatting and cover design infused this book with the sparkle and professionalism that it deserves.

I'd like to give some love to my friend Donna Patterson. Thank you for your generous spirit and liberating perspective. The world is better for you being in it.

A loving thanks to those of you who are a part of this story and inspire me every day. My life, and this book, would be very different if you were not in it. Thanks for the stories, the love and the adventures!

Finally, I would like to acknowledge Spirit. My life has meaning because I have discovered the thread that connects us to each other and to everything else that is real in this world. May everyone who picks up this book receive a blessing from God in whatever form heals your heart and nourishes your soul.

Other Books

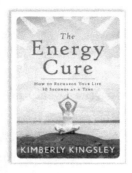

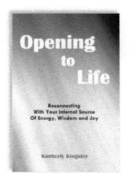

By Kimberly Kingsley